"I had to learn my first lessons in freedom in the most 'un-free' spot in all the world— death row in the Ohio State Pen."

| 0 | 8 | 3 | 2 | 8 | 4 |

Nick the Greek Pirovolos is the executive director of Inside Out, Inc. He and his wife, Dorothy, live in Broadview Hts., Ohio.

William Proctor, a graduate of Harvard Law School and a former criminal court reporter for the *New York Daily News*, is a free-lance writer living and working in New York City.

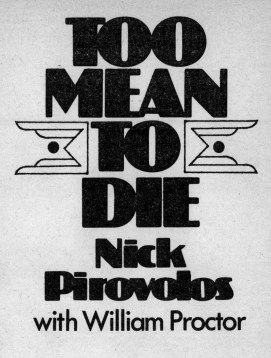

TOO MEAN TO DIE

Nick Pirovolos

with William Proctor

LIVING BOOKS
Tyndale House Publishers, Inc.
Wheaton, Illinois

Second printing, November 1982
Library of Congress Catalog Card Number 81-53034
ISBN 0-8423-7283-0
Copyright © 1982 by Nick Pirovolos and William Proctor
Printed in the United States of America

CONTENTS

1
Out of Control

I had been on a fast track for a long time. My life was filled with big money, beautiful women, and the bright red blood of anybody who dared to get in my way.

But despite the blinding pace of life, I still had the sense of having a hand on the throttle. I could influence the fate of my friends and enemies. I could select my own special brand of thrills and excitement. And most important, I could choose my crimes.

Then things careened out of control. I suppose if I had been older or more experienced, I might have seen what was happening to me. But that wasn't to be. It's like when you're in a car that's plunging off the edge of the road at 100 miles per hour. You can always look back and say, "I guess maybe I should have slowed down at that last turn." But that doesn't get you back on the road or prevent the inevitable crash. And that's exactly what I was headed for — a massive personal pileup that would shake me to the very roots of my cocky Greek being and change my future forever.

The final countdown started at an unlikely spot—a pinball machine in a Cleveland bar. I was playing the machine, and this big, heavy guy walked up to me and asked, "You want to bet a little on that?"

"Sure," I said. I knew he was a pimp who made the rounds from state to state with his girls, moving from one town to the next when the heat from the police got too intense. But he didn't know me—and he certainly didn't know I had practically been born on that machine.

I won twenty dollars from him on the first game. Then $100 on the next. I kept on winning, and soon I had all his money, though I didn't realize it until later.

"Double or nothing," he said.

I said okay, and won again.

"Double or nothing again, but this time we don't touch the machine," he said.

"Fine," I said. I could tell by now he was in trouble, but I wanted to get his last cent, and I knew how to tap that machine on the sly, just as I let the ball go.

He went first and had a fairly good run. But then on my turn, I put that ball out there in the middle—with my secret little tap—and it just didn't want to quit.

The pimp saw I was a sure winner, so rather than let me walk away with all his money, he started in on me: "Why, you cheatin', skinny Greek, you. . . ."

"Yeah, you keep talking, slick. And I'm going to make you a little heavier than you are right now," I said, feeling for the pistol in my back pocket.

"Hey, Greek," Sam the bartender yelled. "No more here. Step outside and take care of your business."

I knew without a doubt I was going to have to shoot this guy. So just as we stepped outside I reached for the little .25 caliber pistol I kept in my pocket. But I was late. Before I could shake the gun loose, he had turned around, stuck a big German Luger in my face, and pulled the trigger.

But nothing happened. There was just a click, no explosion. Now, things like this had happened to me often enough that I was beginning to think I had some kind of invisible shield around me. I didn't waste any time patting myself on the back, though. I grabbed for his gun and his Adam's apple at the same time. And then my luck ran out. He jerked his gun hand loose and whacked me as hard as he could on the top of my head with the barrel. That was when the Luger finally went off. It sounded like a cannon, and the bullet plowed a groove right across the top of my skull.

The blood gushed over both of us, but I kept wrestling with him until I finally rolled on top. I was just about to let him have it with a fist when thirty private detectives and city police arrived.

I was well known among the cops. Some of them were even my friends — at least, they were friendly because I had paid them off on occasion in the past.

"Whose gun is it?" one cop asked.

"It ain't mine," the guy replied. "It's his," he said, pointing at me.

But I lifted up his shirt, and there was his empty Luger holster, big as life for anyone to see.

"Just leave me alone with him for a couple more minutes," I asked the cops. But they wouldn't let me get near him. I could wait to get even. I *always* got even. (Thirty days later, I caught him just after they released him from jail, and I worked him over well enough so that he couldn't walk away so easy. I also took his fourteen prostitutes away from him.)

As the cops drove off with the pimp, I realized my head was still bleeding, so I went back into the bar to look for something to clean myself up with. All I could find was a dirty bar rag they had been using to mop out ashtrays. The barmaid almost fainted when she saw the blood all over me, but I just said, "Don't worry, sweetheart, this is nothing. I'm Nick the Greek. I eat bullets for breakfast and knives for lunch. Everything is cool."

But I didn't feel so cool after I got into the washroom and locked the door behind me. As I washed my head off, the whole sink turned red with blood. The bleeding finally slowed down a little, but then I found I was having some trouble hearing. So I shook my head, but the motion started the wound gushing like a geyser again.

I knew I had to do something fast to patch myself up or I'd pass out, so I walked outside, hailed a cab, and gave my mother's address. The driver didn't notice anything was wrong with me at first. I guess he figured I had put too much grease on my head to keep my curly black hair down. But I must have gotten excited during the ride because the head wound started spouting blood again, and this time the driver *did* notice. As he hit the brake and eyeballed me through his rearview mirror, he said, "Get out of my cab!"

I pulled my pistol out, stuck it against his head, and said, "You're going to take me home."

"No I'm not!" he replied and pointed at a big building outside the car. It was a police station. I didn't want any more trouble than I already had, so I put my gun back in my hip pocket, got out of the cab, and walked as straight as I could to a nearby bar.

I ordered a drink, but that didn't help much. I knew I wasn't going to be able to stay conscious much longer, so I turned to a shaggy-haired, hippie-type guy standing next to me and said, "Brother, I got hurt and need your help. Can you take me home?"

I lucked out because it turned out the guy had a heart. He agreed to help. I gave him some money for a cab, and that's all I remember. The next thing I knew, I was waking up in my mother's home, lying in a bed that was soaked with blood.

Somehow I managed to make it downstairs where my mother was talking to my sister, Irene, who had just come over from Greece. I guess they hadn't known I was upstairs because my mom almost fainted when she saw me.

"What happened?" she gasped.

But I didn't feel like going into detail. In my twenty-four years, she had put up with a lot of things from me, and she had learned at some point it didn't pay to ask too many questions.

"Can you do anything with it?" I asked her. Irene said she thought I should go right to the hospital. But I was more afraid of hospitals and doctors than I was of flying bullets. I didn't trust doctors fooling with my body. And I didn't want my name on any hospital records.

Mom understood how I felt, and she knew there was no point in arguing with me. So she got her scissors and some iodine and started cutting away the clumps of hair matted with dried blood. Her first aid helped some, but the real problem was that the bullet had creased my skull and left a long gouge there that she couldn't fix. So even though the bleeding stopped for a while, I was still in bad shape. During the next few days I lost my sense of taste, and the pain in my head got so bad that I started looking for anything to ease it — morphine, speed, booze, *anything* that would give me a few moments of physical peace.

The only way I could maintain the drug habit I developed over the next few weeks was to steal. And the best places to pick up a lot of cash through quick stickups were some of the local bookie joints and after-hour bars. Unfortunately, the mob bigs that owned those places weren't too understanding. They learned I was behind the robberies, and they put out an open contract on me. That meant any freelance hit men who wanted to could pick up a quick buck by wasting me wherever and whenever they found me. I had become fair game for all the human-hunters of the mob.

It didn't take long for me to realize I was a marked man. I was driving along in this big Chrysler with two big toughs sitting beside me. We were all armed and on the lookout for a store or bookie place to knock over. I hoped these henchmen of mine weren't going to be all hot air. I had met many more big talkers than big actors in my day. At any rate, I kept a close eye on them because I had learned never to trust anybody.

We spotted a likely place. I was about to stop when I glanced up into my rearview mirror and saw a couple of guys in a car just behind us. Something didn't look quite right about them. For one thing, they seemed to be watching us too closely. Also, one guy was black and another white, and this "salt and pepper" combination was a little too unusual in that section of Cleveland.

Relying on the animal instincts I'd developed over the years, I shouted, "Something's up!" and stepped on the gas. It's a good thing, too, because at almost the same time, one of the guys on our tail stuck a chrome pistol out of his window and started firing at us. Now, things were happening so fast there was no time to think. Before I knew it, we were barreling along at 115 miles per hour, sometimes on the wrong side of the two-lane street, sometimes even on the sidewalk. The two guys with me, who had been telling me how tough they were, had fallen completely apart. All the one in the back seat could do was to whine over and over, "Oh, Greek, please stop the car — you'll get us killed!" The other was crouching on the floorboard of the front seat, deep in prayer.

As for me, I got so excited the blood started to gush out of my head again and ran down my face so much I could hardly see. At one point, the hit men pulled right up beside us and when I looked to my left, I found myself staring down the barrel of a big pistol. I'm sure the thug pulled the trigger, but nothing happened. Another misfire had saved me.

I pulled out ahead of them again, but then my luck ran out. The gunmen shot my right rear tire. I went into this spin and slammed into a parked Rambler. I was knocked half senseless and couldn't even turn my head as I saw out of the corner of my eye the two hit men walking toward me. Blood poured out of my eyes, nose, and mouth, and I had been shot through one of my hands. I remember the thugs were both wearing blue suits, and they looked real efficient and businesslike. One yanked my car door open, stuck his gun in my face, and pulled the trigger. But once again, nothing happened. These misfires were getting to be a regular part of my life.

But the fists and feet and a couple of pipes wielded by the two hit men didn't misfire. They punched me so hard and so often I stopped feeling any pain. My eyes were almost completely closed now, and I couldn't even defend myself, much less carry the fight to them.

"Oh, God," I thought. "What a cheap way to die." And I slipped to the ground, still holding one of the guy's coat lapels.

The police came right at that moment. If they'd come a minute later, I wouldn't have lived to tell you about it. The cops waded through the crowd of people that had been watching the show, grabbed me and rushed me straight to the hospital. But like I said, I don't like hospitals. And I heal pretty fast. So as bad as I was still feeling and as much as I was still bleeding, I checked myself out of the hospital that same night, picked up a pistol and went out to take care of some unfinished business that was bugging me — getting even with the two thugs who had done this to me.

I tried several spots I figured they might be hanging out, and I finally found them in a pool hall. I yelled out to them, just to let them know that the Greek had come back. Then I let fly with a hailstorm of bullets. I don't know how much damage I did. But I do know I had this warm, satisfied feeling inside me that the scales of Greek justice had tipped once again in my favor.

But that good feeling didn't last long. My head soon started hurting again, this time from a concussion I'd suffered, and now it was worse than ever. I needed even more drugs and medicine, and that meant holding up more stores and after-hour joints.

Then came what I thought was not only my chance to solve my medical problems, but to take a ride on easy street for a while as well. I got a small gang together to hit a grocery store in a little town outside Cleveland. We had heard that the owners of this place had big money in a safe there, and I figured that with my cut I could pay for a lot of painkillers and have plenty of good times besides. So I threw together a quick plan, got a pistol and a few knives, and headed out to the store with these three other guys.

The holdup went real smoothly. We walked in on the store manager, and our plan proceeded without a hitch. We were in and out of the place in a few minutes. But there were a couple of things that made the job less than perfect. For one thing, there wasn't any big money. My cut was only $368. I often spent more than that on dinner for my friends at nice restaurants, or on a new suit of clothes.

And there was another little problem. As we sat in

the car splitting our nickle-dime take, our driver glanced up in the rearview mirror and saw a couple of squad cars bearing down on us. We took off like a bunch of wild men and managed to keep ahead of them until we reached a nearby interstate. Now, I figured, they wouldn't have a chance to catch us — not with Nick the Greek directing the getaway.

It was about then that I saw them — eighteen more squad cars parked in a massive horseshoe formation just in front of us, blocking the highway. And behind us, where there had been only two police cars, there were now four or five. We were trapped.

"Let's have a shoot-out," one of my brighter men said. I looked at him like he was crazy.

"You got to be kidding," I said. "We've only got one gun."

I managed to get rid of the gun before they arrested us, but they still charged us with several counts of armed robbery and concealed weapons. You see, I forgot to ditch my stiletto knives.

It was a big deal for me to finally end up in jail. The police had been trying to nail me with something for years. Five Ohio counties took part in the arraignments because they all wanted a hand in my arrest. The courtroom was packed with spectators and reporters, and I heard a radio blaring in a courthouse hallway, "Flash! Nick the Greek, armed robber and terrorizer, has been captured. . . ."

I didn't really believe my arrest was going to change things much, though. For one thing, I didn't expect to spend much time behind bars. Also, while I was in jail, I still expected to rule the roost.

When I first walked into the county jail, an inmate "trusty," a trusted prisoner who helped out with official administration, came over to me and said, "You get cell number seven, but you'll have to sleep on the floor because there ain't enough bunks."

I looked at him kind of hard and said, "No, *you* get the floor because I'm taking over your bunk."

And that's what happened. Just like that. I didn't have time to play with those guys, and I had a way of making other people feel afraid of me. I had been shot in the head and through the hand, pistol-whipped, and punched and kicked, and I wasn't in any mood for tea and crumpets. I walked into that jail like an animal because I knew it was important to make your power play right at the beginning. When the lions start to growl, the toughest lion has to growl the loudest. And that's what I did.

But the guards still had ultimate power over me, and they wanted to make me hurt. So they kept my medicines away from me. I needed enough painkiller to stop an elephant, yet they only allotted me one lousy pill each day. So I struck out the only way I knew how. Although they had taken everything out of my cell but my mattress, I set it on fire with some matches I had hidden away. They slapped a couple of counts of arson on me for that, but I wasn't about to let them get the last blow in. As the sheriff was walking by my cell one day, I reached out, grabbed him by the neck, and started to choke him.

The official response was to put a mean-looking weight lifter in my cell with me. This inmate, who always wore a smelly Mickey Mouse T-shirt, was supposed to be a kind of enforcer, who imposed order on unruly prisoners in return for certain favors from the guards. He didn't jump me right away, though. I could see he was sizing me up, biding his time.

The first day I let him do his thing, and he kept his distance from me. But the second day he started playing his Mickey Mouse games with me. I always like my coffee in the morning, so when the jail trusty came by with a couple of big buckets, I started to stick my tin cup through the bars to get some.

But the weight lifter said, "No. *I'm* running this thing now."

But when he opened his mouth to say that, I was already prepared for him. I looked straight into his face to get his attention, but my cup was turning at the same time in my hand so that I was holding the bottom of it with the sharp upper lip facing out. He never knew what hit him because I never gave him a chance. I caught him right on the temple with the edge of that cup, and as he staggered backward, I started butting him on the face with my head.

We call this kind of fighting "coco-butting," I guess because you try to crack the other guy's head open like a coconut. This way of mixing it up always hurt me, but it hurt the other guy a lot more. Also, I didn't really care if I got hurt, and that made me doubly scary in a fight. Pretty soon, his whole face was bleeding. The jail guards, who were watching the whole thing on a closed-circuit TV camera, didn't stop it at first because they thought the weight lifter would beat me up. But when it became obvious that *I* was the one who was doing the beating, the guards came in with their clubs and hard hats and stopped it.

That night, just to show them I was still in good shape, I convinced all the guys on my side to stick their blankets down the toilets, so my whole side of the jail got flooded. "I'm Nick 'Persaw,' the devil's son-in-law!" I yelled when they came in to clean things up. Not such a great rhyme, maybe, but they got the point.

At first, I told my lawyer I wanted to plead not guilty to everything so they'd have to hold a jury trial on each of the charges against me. I wanted to make them pay. But then the prosecutor showed me a movie that had been taken of us holding up the grocery store. I didn't know there had been a camera on us, but there I was, big as life, waving a pistol around during the armed robbery. I just smiled during the last part of the film. "They got me," I told my lawyer.

So I decided to plead guilty. But I wasn't really very worried. The judge knew I was sick, with all those bullet holes in me. That had to be worth a little sympathy. Also, I had never spent any long period of time in jail before. And if none of this moved the judge, surely he had heard of my family. He must know he could get paid off if he wanted. Or he or his family could get worked over pretty nice if he didn't fall in line.

I was confident when I walked into the courtroom for my sentencing. I wore a pink shirt and maroon tie because I had already picked the restaurant and bar where I'd celebrate when they released me.

I strolled up with my cocky little strut to face the judge at the bench. When I looked into his eyes, I started to lose some of my confidence. "Young man, I've been a judge for twenty-five years, and you are the very first Greek who has stood before me," the judge said. "So I am going to make an example of you. I sentence you to ten to twenty-five years in prison."

I couldn't believe it. My mind went completely blank. This couldn't really be happening to Nick the Greek. I had done plenty of things worse than this two-bit armed robbery, but all I'd got before was a slap on the wrist. Didn't this judge know that, despite all the trouble I'd been causing in the jail, I was a sick man? I could hardly walk from one side of the courtroom to the other without getting a splitting headache and nearly passing out. Didn't he know it was going to cost the state more in hospital bills to keep me in prison than it would if he just let me go?

But I could see this judge wasn't about to change his mind. And that's when I started to get really scared. I began to think about the Mansfield prison where I would be sent. I had a lot of enemies there — a lot of guys I had knifed and shot and beat up.

And my fears didn't subside when I finally saw the prison from the truck they used to transport me. The driver took an extra long time to get there, and when I asked him about that, he said, "We know you probably got some guys waiting on the regular route to hijack us, Greek. So we ain't taking no chances."

Actually, I didn't have anybody waiting on the regular route. But I decided that if I ever came this way again, I'd see what I could do not to disappoint my next driver. In the meantime, though, I had plenty to keep me occupied. The mean-looking gun towers and forty-foot high walls of Mansfield had appeared on the horizon, and my fear turned into panic. Even though I could play a tough-guy role well, I knew I wasn't superman. I had beat up on a lot of people in my day, but one reason for my success was that I often used an "equalizer" — a hidden knife, brass knuckles, or a gun. It wasn't so easy to get the kind of weapons I liked in jail.

Not only that, but as I looked down at myself, I was reminded I am actually a rather small man. I often assumed I was a giant. But I was really kind of short, and I weighed only about 130 pounds. I had found in the past I could rely on surprise and cocky self-confidence to win over bigger opponents. But now, as I neared those prison walls, I sensed the rules of the game were about to change.

There was another fear which I had always pushed out of my mind before, but which I now knew I was going to have to face directly. I had heard there were only two types of guys who survived in prison: those who walked around rough and tough and scared their enemies off or crushed them; and the homosexuals and "slaves" who serviced the tough guys.

I wasn't sure I was big or healthy enough at this

point to be a successful tough guy. But I was *absolutely* sure of one thing: I knew I would never become a slave or a homosexual. In fact, the more I thought about it, the madder I got. "If I'm going to die in there, at least I'll take a few of them with me," I muttered to myself. So I pushed all those fears down inside me and walked into Mansfield on a wave of hate.

And I needed that hate to keep me going as I was processed that first day. Every prison is ugly, and Mansfield was no exception. There were tough-looking guards all over the place, with ugly uniforms and billy clubs. They had built gun towers *inside* the prison, so they could shoot inmates who started riots. Everywhere I went, I saw dull gray walls, cages, and bars, and I felt my aching head being jarred down to my spine as the metal cell doors clanged open and shut around me.

As for the inmates, they *all* looked like they were sizing me up, like that weight lifter in the county jail. None of them smiled. Smiling was a sign you were weak or a homosexual. They just stared holes in me, like wild animals studying their prey's most vulnerable spot before an attack. I was a "fish," or new boy, and everybody was waiting to see where I'd fit in — or *if* I'd fit in.

On that very first day, I saw a few guys I had known on the outside. Some had been allies, others enemies. But I wasn't quite prepared for what happened when I finally got assigned to a cell on the lowest tier and plopped down on my rack for a little shut-eye, to ease that headache I still had from my gunshot wound and beatings.

Before I could even close my eyes, I heard some guy on the next tier of cells yell, "Hey, Greek, swing with the doors!"

I sat bolt upright and asked my "celly," or cellmate, "What does that mean?"

"It means there's going to be a war between you and him," my celly explained. "He'll be waiting for you when his doors open in the morning."

I didn't know who this guy was, and I had no idea what I had done to him in the past. Not only that, I had never played this particular prison game before. But they didn't call me treacherous for nothing. Whenever I was threatened, I always relied on surprise and dirty tricks. And I knew that was exactly what was called for in this case.

So I got the attention of one of the other inmates I had known on the outside — a "range boy" who brought water to the other inmates at night. He had the run of some of the prison shops, and he agreed to slip me a big can of lighter fluid that night. My cell door was one of the first opened for breakfast in the morning, but instead of going directly to the mess hall with the other inmates, I lagged behind with my lighter fluid and some matches I'd managed to get from another inmate. When the way was clear, I climbed to the next tier and found the cell of the guy who had yelled that challenge at me.

He was still asleep under his blanket, and I thought, "Sweet dreams, sucker!" as I sprayed him and his mattress with the lighter fluid. As he finally started to wake up, I yelled, "Here I am!" I could tell by the terrified look on his face, as he stared into the grin I was giving him, that he knew what was coming. I sprayed some more lighter fluid on him just for good measure. Then I lit the match.

The flames were all around him in a matter of seconds, and I left him screaming and beating the fire out with his other blankets. I went on down to breakfast as though nothing had happened, and the prison officials never found out who was responsible. He lived, but he learned his lesson. And the word got around among the other inmates. They knew not to mess around with me after that.

With such a successful spree of violence my first day, I might have been well on my way to becoming one of the prison's godfathers. But I was a very sick young man. I tried to be mean, but I often got dizzy and even passed out once from the head wound.

And that wasn't my only problem. The left side of my face, where I had been pistol-whipped, had become so sensitive I couldn't stand to be out in the winter air or even to touch my injured cheek. Every time I coughed, I coughed blood. I also started to lose my sense of balance and taste, and I began staying in my cell instead of going out for food or the other inmate activities.

One of the friendlier guards, who had noticed I was acting funny, said, "What's the matter, Greek?" I wasn't used to asking anybody for help, but I knew I had to get some medical help soon or I wouldn't last much longer in the prison jungle. The strong devour the weak in prison, and I was getting weaker by the day. So, against my usual nature, I opened up to the guard, and, to my relief, he immediately offered to help.

The guard took me to the prison hospital, where they arranged for some X-rays. It was decided my condition was so bad I'd have to go to the intensive care ward at the Ohio State Penitentiary. So they sent me to the Ohio State Pen where some other doctors took some more X-rays. And all the time I was getting more and more scared. It seemed as if most of the time I was standing around in my underwear, getting ready for somebody to stick a needle in me here, poke me with some instrument there, or take another picture of my cracked-up insides. The doctors kept talking about putting me on the operating table and cutting into my skull, and a question that kept coming up was, "Hey, Greek, you want to sign this sheet so your eyeballs will be donated to science if something happens to you when you go under the knife?"

No, I didn't want to donate my eyeballs! And I didn't want to undergo an operation, either. But I knew I was in bad shape because I still had great pain, and every time I coughed, some blood would come up. I didn't know if I was dying, but I did know I needed help. The question I had was, did these doctors really want to help me? For that matter, *could* they help me? And could I trust them?

With all these doubts and worries on my mind, I wasn't in any mood to make friends — especially not with the strange little Mexican inmate who always seemed to show up to take my X-rays. He always had this big smile on his face, and I thought he was either a homosexual or a bandit out to get what little possessions I had left. As I said before, nobody smiles in prison unless he's a little strange.

"What's happening, brother?" the Mexican asked me one day.

I got very wise right away. "Hey," I said. "I don't have a brother in here, and I never knew my father got to Mexico."

I wanted to cut him off, let him know I wasn't playing any games. But he turned around and said, "We're all brothers! In Jesus Christ!"

I couldn't believe my ears. This guy was talking about God on Wednesday instead of Sunday. I thought maybe he was a priest, but he was wearing a white hospital coat, so I started looking for a crucifix or something that would put him in the clergy. But there was nothing like that on him.

"My name is Ernie, and they call me 'Super-Mex!' " he said.

"Okay, okay." I tried to shut him up by ignoring him.

But then he got more interesting. He asked, "Do you want freedom?"

"How much?" I asked almost without thinking. "How much would it cost me?" I did want freedom because by this time I had gotten a dear John letter from my old girlfriend. I hadn't treated her too well, and she wanted some revenge for all the bad things I'd done to her. Not only that, I was scared to death of the prison doctors. And I had heard the immigration people might be after me to send me back to Greece because they had decided I was an undesirable and a menace to society, a person who had committed moral turpitude — whatever that was — against the American people. So yes, I definitely did want freedom, to escape from the pressures of the prison, settle some old scores, and pick up my old life on the outside again.

But that wasn't what Super-Mex had in mind. He said, "Freedom is when you allow Jesus Christ to come into your heart."

Now, I knew God was Greek, so how could this heathen, this unbeliever, tell me about the God we Greeks had created? What did he know? Mexico was not as old as Greece! But there was something different about this Mexican, something I couldn't put my finger on right away. He was certainly different from the other inmates I knew. In the few weeks I'd been in prison, I had got used to having guys come in, sit on my bunk, and talk about what life used to be like in the old days when they were on the outside. But in the meantime, they were smoking my cigarettes and eating my candy bars. They wanted to talk, but they also wanted to get something off me. But this Mexican wasn't trying to put on the dog, or put something over on me. His eyes told me he was real. Something inside me said, "This guy has got something I wish I could get." But then another voice said, "I'm Nick the Greek, and I know only chickens and homosexuals and old ladies and little kids turn to God."

But there was something true about what this guy was saying. His words reminded me of the Bible passages my mother had read to me as a kid and the stories about God my grandmother had told on the flat rooftop of our house in Greece as we lay around in the cool evening air just before we went to bed. Finally, though, I decided I was probably too far gone to change my way of life now; and besides, what would my friends say if I gave my life to Jesus in the way he was talking about?

But the Mexican kept working on me until finally I had to tell him, "Shut up! I don't want to hear about your God! Just let me do my time. I'm a convict, and that's what I want to be. I want to be a good convict, and I don't want to hear nothing more about God."

But I was still scared. I was feeling as bad as ever. I couldn't understand half of what the doctors were trying to tell me because my English wasn't so good. They kept shooting needles in me, in my thighs and shoulders and rear. My skin got so tough, they could hardly get the shots in me sometimes. They took me to some kind of therapy every day and hung me in traction from the neck up, but it never seemed to do any good. In fact, at one point the pain got so bad—I was in such a living hell—that I actually paid a guy two cartons of cigarettes, or $2.65, to kill me. But he didn't live up to his part of the bargain. You couldn't trust anybody, it seemed.

I cursed the doctors all the time, but that didn't seem to do any good either. I felt like a guinea pig because all these specialists kept coming in and looking at me for a few minutes without doing anything to help me. They seemed to get a big kick out of showing me my X-rays: "Now, this is where you were cut on the left eye, and that's where the guy shot you with the pistol. . . ." But none of the talk did a thing to ease the pain I felt. If I even got touched on some parts of my head, the pain would be so bad I'd pass out.

The only way I found to get my mind off my own problems was to get into some of the criminal activities that go on in every prison. Since I was in the hospital, I had access to drugs other people didn't, so I started dealing a little dope to the other inmates, in exchange for underwear, towels, or whatever else I might need. Sometimes I even traded my own medicines if I wasn't hurting too bad myself some days.

I also tried to make some useful underworld contacts that I thought might help me in prison and also later, when I was released. One of the top dogs I had known on the outside was in the Ohio Pen while I was in the hospital there. He was so bad he had started a riot in the prison and had killed several people with a sledgehammer. He managed to get into the hospital to see me by swallowing some iodine and gauze so the prison authorities would admit him.

But despite all my efforts to submerge myself in the criminal world of the prison, I somehow couldn't get away from Ernie, the Mexican. "Hey, Greek-o, how you doing?" he'd say almost every day with a big smile when he passed my bunk.

Some of the other inmates would see him coming and say, "Oh, no, here comes that Jesus freak, that homosexual."

But I also learned these same guys wouldn't say that to Ernie's face because he was a top-rated boxer in his weight class and could have made mincemeat out of any of us in a fair fight. When Ernie wasn't grinning, he was singing songs like "Amazing Grace" and "The Old Rugged Cross," which I'd never heard before. We never sang tunes like that in the Greek Orthodox Church. These tunes had a catchy lilt to them, and, against my better judgment, I found myself whistling the same tunes myself.

"Hey, Greek, God can give you freedom," the Mexican kept saying, and even though I had taken to not answering him, a war was raging inside me. When the Mexican spoke to me, I kept on hearing my grandmother in Greece, I remembered I had once wanted to be a priest, and I saw what an animal I had become.

Then one day I started taking an inventory of my life. It was like a tape had started playing in my brain, a tape I had no power to shut off. What have I done with my life? I asked. I looked down at myself and saw that the only thing I owned was the socks I was wearing. Even my underwear, which was full of holes, belonged to the state. I didn't even have a name. I was a number — inmate 83284.

All my life, I had only been out for myself. And I'd learned to enjoy hurting other people. I always returned bad for good. Even the Mexican inmate Ernie, who had been trying to share his religion with me, got the back of my hand. The only thing he ever asked of me was to teach him how to speak some Greek so he could read parts of the Bible in the original language. But I had just taught him Greek curse words until finally he caught on to what I was doing. When I finally did teach him the "Our Father" to get him to stop pestering me, he put my words on tape and slept with it playing in his ear. The very next day, he came in speaking Greek with my accent.

But if I'd done little for Ernie, I'd done even less for my own mother, who had tried to love me and who stuck by me even after all the crimes I'd committed.

Some others in my family tried to see me once, but it didn't work out. They all had their own lives to live. And after all, I had done a lot of hurt to them.

My mother was the only one who had visited me since I'd been sent to prison. But even though she let me know she still loved me, she didn't pull any punches about how much I'd hurt her. She said, "Son, I've prayed to Almighty God that you would stay here for the rest of your life. That you would rot in jail. That you would never get out and hurt anybody else again."

It was tough, hearing words like that from my own mother. But I knew she was just telling the truth. Looking deep into her sad eyes, I remembered those times when I'd come home stinking drunk, and as she would go to help me take my clothes off, I'd kick her. One day I kicked her right in the mouth without knowing what I was doing, and when I came down for breakfast the next morning, I saw she was all black and blue. I asked her what happened, and she said something about slipping down and falling against a door handle.

"At least when you're in jail, I'll know you're alive — and you're not hurting anyone else," she said. Those were her last words to me before she left, and they were eating away at my mind.

So this tape kept playing in my mind, this record of my past life, and I didn't like what I saw. I was a total drain on society and my family. I had hated my father for his cruelty, but now I was ten times worse. I had become an animal, a no-good. I stank, physically and morally. I put a dirty smudge on every woman I touched. I had made enough money to retire in style — if I hadn't spent it all on dope and booze and high living. I had learned to sleep with my gun cocked under my pillow, and it's a wonder I hadn't shot my own brains away. As a matter of fact, I had been shot and wounded by other people four different times, and I realized that if any of those bullets had killed me, society could easily have done without me. I wouldn't have been missed.

I used to brag that a mean old dog I owned and I had places prepared in hell next to each other. I had really sold my soul to Satan. So I asked myself, "Can God really forgive me? I think I'm too far gone."

But something in me seemed to say, "No you're not too far gone. Just like the thief on the cross was not too far gone."

This argument kept raging inside me, and I wondered to myself, "Can God hear me while I'm lying around here in my bed? Maybe I should get down on my knees if I'm really going to have a chance to hear him if he should want to say something to me."

Then I thought, "Wait just a minute! There are thirty-two other guys here in this hospital ward. What are they gonna think if I get down on my knees now? It's broad daylight, and every one of them will see me!"

But I knew something important was happening inside me, and I didn't want to take any chances that God wouldn't have his say — if he had anything at all to say to me. So I finally got up enough courage to crawl out of my bed and kneel on the floor, just as I used to do as a little boy in Greece.

The other inmates noticed right away something strange was happening, and the catcalls and sarcasm started almost immediately. "Hey, Greek, you lose something down there?" "Hey, Greek, you losing your nerve?" "Hey, Greek, are you trying to get religion?"

I heard them, all right. And the thought did cross my mind, "Just what *am* I doing down here?"

But then the tape in my brain—that mental recording of my past life—kept playing louder and louder until I wasn't aware of what those inmates were saying to me. All I heard or saw were those early years, when I had been a little boy on the island of Chios in Greece. . . .

Roots

I should have had a happy boyhood. On the Greek island of Chios where I was born, the weather always seemed to be perfect. It was never too cold to go outside to play, and we never seemed to run out of tangerines, oranges, almonds, and olives on the trees around our home.

I had my own little donkey to ride. What kid doesn't dream of that? And the physical setting I grew up in was matchless for a child, with clear blue water nearby and a craggy peak we called "Grandma Mountain" close enough to take hikes to when we were in the mood to play mountain climber.

The people in my corner of Greece were fascinating too. We had some of the wealthiest people in the world who lived on that little island, and even the ordinary folks lived better than most. There was never any reason to want for anything if you lived on Chios. The people of the past were always present with us too, to inspire us and make us proud. Hardly a week went by when I didn't hear some reference to Socrates, Hercules, or Ulysses.

As I said, I should have been happy as a boy. But I wasn't. I had one of the most miserable childhoods you can imagine, and the main reason for my unhappiness was my father.

Now, I know what I'm about to tell you may make me look like an ungrateful son. You may even think I'm stooping so low as to tell terrible lies about my own father. But as God is my witness, every word I'm about to relate to you is true.

On their wedding night, my father beat my mother up. That's how their marriage got started, and things went downhill from then on. As far back as I can remember, my father was always whipping somebody in the family when he was at home. Lucky for us, he was gone to sea as a merchant for several months at a time. But when he returned to Chios, we caught it.

Once when he came home, he grabbed a loaf of bread we had in the cupboard and put a little nick on the end of it with his knife. "This is how much you're going to eat tonight," he said to my mom. But if she and the seven kids living at home had tried to get along on that thin slice, there would have been a lot of empty stomachs in our house that day.

So Mom decided to disobey him. She put another nick like the one he had made, but farther down on the loaf, to give us all a little more food that evening. But when my father got home he went right to the bread, examined it, and shouted, "This is not the nick I made! You weren't supposed to eat this much!"

And he proceeded to beat my mother as we huddled in the center of the room crying, knowing we would be next. We may have gotten a little more nourishment that day, but we paid for it dearly with bruises and blood. And unlike the family situation in the United States, there was no such thing as talking back to your parents in Greece. If it was night outside and your father said it was day, then it was day — even if you knew it was night.

The way my father tried to deprive us of the basic things of life, like food, you'd have thought we were a poor family. But actually, he made plenty of money on his business trips. Sometimes, it seemed to me there was absolutely no family love, no normal human sentiment in my dad. Most adults melt at the sweet smile of a pretty little girl who is just starting to walk. But when my baby sister was that age, he kicked her so hard she sprawled out on the floor crying.

If you heard the *whole* story of my early life, you would get sick; and you should be aware that just remembering it, living through it again in my mind, makes me sick too. But it's an important story if you hope to understand how I developed into the kind of person I did. As much as I hated and feared him, my father was my role model for what an adult male was like. I didn't like what I saw, but as the years wore on, it became easier and easier for me to conform to the mold that had been set by him.

I've often puzzled over why my mother married my dad, but I've never come up with a satisfying answer. I know she had reached marriageable age, and she and my grandmom felt it was time to bring a man into the house. That's the way you did things in Greece. But exactly why they brought this particular man in — well, that's something I've never quite been able to figure out. But once the wedding bells had grown still, my mom found she had literally made a very uncomfortable bed and was going to have to learn to lie in it. More than a dozen kids came out of that stormy union, and nine survived, all with some emotional or physical scars that they would have to carry into adult life.

But the family members weren't the only ones who

suffered from my father's mean temper. He was a man who seemed to be motivated primarily by revenge or by money, and he was happiest when he was in hot pursuit of one of those goals. He gained a reputation in Chios as the kind of guy who would stop at nothing to settle a score if he felt he had been wronged. For example, he loved hot white bread, and we had a small bakery in our village that produced some of the best. One day, when my dad was in the bakery, he got into an argument with the baker.

My father finally said, "You take back your words, or I make you lick my shoes!"

The baker refused to back down, so my father went to another island and returned with another baker and a lot of flour. He built an old broken-down oven and set up a bakery where he produced bread that he actually gave away to the villagers. Even though the other baker was selling his loaves for only two or three cents, he couldn't beat my father's price, which was no price at all.

All this time, my father's kids, including me, were at home with too little to eat and not even enough money to buy shoes. And there he was, sitting on a big brown horse he owned, with woven baskets full of bread slung over the back of the saddle, giving it away to whomever walked past him on the street. I know my father ultimately won that argument with our town's baker. I even heard he actually had that man licking his shoes, just so my father would close up his free bakery. So our immediate family members weren't the only ones who suffered from my father's vindictive nature.

But like I said, revenge was only one of the things that made him tick. Something that turned him on even more was money, and it seemed he was willing to stop at nothing to enrich himself just a little more, here and there.

As a little boy I was told over and over by people inside and outside the family that my father could pick up a piece of garbage and turn it into gold. He could stand on a rock and make money. That was the kind of reputation he had. And I had countless object lessons in the way he went about living his life. I filed in my little brain the sharp dealings he conducted with others in the marketplace; the violence he inflicted on our family. But at that point I didn't start imitating my father. The seeds of my own rebellion and cruelty had certainly been firmly planted. But the fertile soil in which they were to grow and flourish, to the discomfort and horror of other human beings, didn't appear until a few years later.

During these early years in Greece, I rejected everything my father did and stood for and turned instead to my mother, Despina Pirovolos, whose God-fearing influence actually made me decide that I wanted to be a priest. Her grandfather had been a priest, and she was raised in the constant presence of church tradition. So I guess with that kind of family background, it was natural for me to think about a career in the church. Because my father didn't give us enough money to live on, my mother and all the kids had to go out and get extra jobs. One of the things we loved to do most was serve as church janitors. Our whole clan, minus my father, would go into a church and scour the place from the top to bottom so thoroughly that we got a reputation for being the best in that line of work. Local priests would come to see my mother and try to be sure she plugged their sanctuary into her schedule.

I was also in the church for worship with my brothers and sisters almost every time the doors opened for services. One of my favorite times, though, was Easter, which is the biggest day of celebration in our country. It was like the Fourth of July because when the priests would announce "He is risen!" everybody would shoot off fireworks to express their joy.

But even the Easter season couldn't be completely happy when my father was around. I remember one Palm Sunday, when the rest of the family was heading toward church, we passed a plaza where some of the town tough guys, including my father, were sitting around under a big tree. This particular group of men never went to church, not even on the major holidays. They felt religion was something for women and children, but not for strong, grown men. And my father was the most hostile of all.

I still recall that as we passed him that day he was staring at one of the men of the town who had chosen to attend the services. "May the ceiling fall on him!" my father muttered. That was the kind of man my father was.

But in those early days, as I said, I didn't agree with my father. I was much more drawn to the Bible passages I heard in church and in our home. And the exciting Bible stories my mother and grandmother related about Samson and David and Moses and the other Old Testament patriarchs really captivated me. Some of my fondest memories are of those cool nights when we would sit up on the top of our flat-roofed house with the gentle sea breezes wafting over us and listen to those ancient accounts of how God had shaped history through the individual lives of those heroic old Hebrews. I might have had a hard day for an eight-year-old, either cleaning a big church, or selling lemonade and candy apples in the village on holidays, or enduring one of the many beatings from my father. But those nights on the rooftop, absorbing God's Word in the company of family members who really did love me, was enough to make me ready to face another tough day.

The spiritual world even dominated my play. I was the kind of little guy that if I found a dead animal, I'd give it a whole burial liturgy, like the ones I had seen the priests conduct in church. I'd put together a little casket, get some other young kids to follow me in a funeral procession, and then we'd march down the street, singing hymns.

But there was a dark side to the Greek spiritual world — a side I was also regularly exposed to as a boy. There is a belief in Greece that when a person dies, his spirit wanders around restlessly for forty days. To calm the spirit and send it smoothly to the next world, a tradition has sprung up of lighting candles on the dead person's grave every day for that forty-day period; and poor people are often hired to be sure the candles stay lit.

We were always short of money, and my mom took on this job of lighting the candles in graveyards to bring a few extra coins into our household. She was especially concerned that my sisters would have enough money for a decent dowry when they decided to get married, and a lot of my mom's candle-lighting money went into that fund.

But lighting those candles could really be a creepy business, and Mom sometimes took me along to keep her company. I remember one night we walked through the graveyard until we found the freshly-dug grave where she was to light her candles. Dusk was already turning into the pitch black of night, and I found myself starting at every rustle of leaves or cracking twig. There are a lot of Greek folk superstitions about how witches and demons come out at dusk, and it was easy to believe in them when you were kneeling on the cold ground in front of a new grave. We lit the candle, and I sat there silently for a few moments in the eerie, flickering light that distorted the appearance of everything it touched. I was too petrified to look at anything but the flame at first, but as the seconds wore on, I dared to glance beyond the flame at the trunk of a nearby tree. Then I looked over to my left, where my mother was sitting. Nothing there but a few more graves and shrubs. I was getting so confident now that I looked over to the right with hardly a thought. And that's when I saw it. A human skull staring right at me, with a mocking grin showing through jagged, broken teeth!

I flew back down that hill toward home so fast, I bet my feet never touched ground! My mom was a little put out when she arrived at our house later that night. She explained that the skull I saw was part of some bones that had been dug up from a shallow grave to make room for a new grave that was being prepared. But all the logical explanations in the world couldn't have convinced me to go back to that graveyard again.

Even if my experience in that graveyard could be explained in a rational way, there were other strange contacts with the spirit-world that couldn't be dismissed quite so easily. We Greeks are steeped in Christianity. But we're also steeped in occult, pagan superstitions, and sometimes those superstitions can get the better of us.

One time, a gypsy came to our house in Chios to try to sell us some clothes. As he was laying out his goods, he glanced up at me and looked into my face. And then he froze. "Young man, your eyes!" he exclaimed. "God help women from your eyes. God help people away from your eyes. You're going to destroy lives or be a great man — just because of your eyes. The gift is upon you, and it will come through your eyes!"

That little piece of fortune-telling had a demonic edge to it, because the gypsy's words worked in me all my life. I had learned as a youngster to accept the

38

power of the occult, as well as of God, and I believed, without any reservation, what that wanderer told me. I had some reason to believe in the power of the black arts because I had seen them applied, and I was convinced I had seen them work. One of my distant relatives was deep into witchcraft, and my family was constantly getting involved in situations where she had tried to cast some spell or curse on somebody.

One time, she had it in for some guy in our village, so she nailed a bar of soap on the wall in his basement, where the moisture and urine from goats and other animals caused it to begin to melt away.

"If the soap breaks, his life breaks," she had said in a secret ceremony, and even though the guy had been healthy, he got quite sick and his life seemed to be fading away.

He finally went to the local priest to see if anything could be done that the doctors weren't doing, and after some investigation, the priest found the soap and removed it. The result was that the man immediately started to recover.

Our family wasn't immune to this kind of black magic from this relative, either. She put some strands of hair in the cuffs of one of my brother Gus's pairs of pants, and everytime he wore them he got sick and melancholy. One day when my sister was ironing those pants, she found this clump of hair in the cuff and threw it away. Gus never again had any problem with sickness.

Now some of this occult stuff may not seem so important. After all, you may say, nobody was hurt so bad that they died. But actually, somebody did die — one of my brothers who never lived past his infancy. When this little boy was about a year old, my relative looked at him and told my father, "This baby looks too much like you. One of you is going to die."

Now most people might have been able to laugh off such a prediction, but not my father. He was very interested in his own safety, and he believed in the dark powers.

So when that little boy got very sick a few months later, my mother went to my father and cried, "Go get a doctor!"

But he replied, "No doctor will come into this house!" Then, he went back to sleep.

The baby got worse and worse. And finally, he died, while gazing helplessly at Mom and crying, "Mama, Mama!"

So that's the way I spent my early boyhood, until I was about ten years old. There was hate and love. Fear and comfort. Violence and peacefulness. Pain and innocent play. Satan and God.

But these were just seeds. Nobody, least of all me, knew exactly what they would amount to in the years ahead. Other people, other events, other pressures had to provide the soil in which they would grow to maturity. But that part of my story comes later. For the moment, suffice it to say that my mother and father were finally separated, and then they tried independently to start the bureaucratic wheels rolling so they could immigrate to the United States.

For my mother and all of us children, America had represented a kind of freedom it's hard for native Americans to understand. The United States had always seemed to be a land where anything was possible. I know now there was a lot of myth in that attitude — a lot like the fantasies we in Greece held about our own glorious past. But real or not, we really believed America was the land of opportunity for us, and we became more and more deeply motivated by that belief. It was hard for a woman and a bunch of small kids to make enough money to make ends meet in a relatively primitive economy like Chios had.

So we were seeking economic freedom from the poverty we faced. But we also wanted a kind of emotional freedom from the environment where we had been oppressed so long by my father's presence and reputation. Granted, he and my mother weren't living together anymore. But everywhere we turned, there were unpleasant memories of him. Sometimes, we felt the most important thing in the world was to escape those memories.

But my father was also interested in going to the United States. He had always had a fascination with North America, especially since he sent my oldest brother there. And my brother did quite well for himself. He became a U.S. citizen and turned into quite a hero in the Korean War as a combat soldier.

Most of us in the family were very proud to have such a distinguished relative. But my father's reaction? While my brother was on the front lines in Korea, I can remember my father saying one time: "God, if you're there, kill him so I can collect his $10,000 G.I. insurance!"

My father never seemed to change. So in one way it was a devastating shock, but in another way quite predictable that, when we looked over the list of people who had been approved to emigrate from Greece, my father's name was right there with ours. I remember when my mother read that list and saw his name there, she broke down and cried. But he promised us he had changed and things would be better with a new start in a new country. So she took him in again.

As we boarded that airplane that would fly us into New York, we realized that the perfect freedom we sought was not to be. We did hold out hope that, even with my father present, we might discover a better life than we had known in Chios. But if we had known what a chamber of horrors awaited us on the other side of the Atlantic Ocean, we would probably have headed straight back to our little Greek village and never consider leaving it again.

3

A Land
of Little
Opportunity

Traveling on an airplane isn't any big deal for most middle-class Americans these days. But for me, that flight from Athens to New York City was like being transported on a magic carpet to some sort of fantasy land.

I had never had a real vacation before. Much of my ten years of life, especially in the recent past, had involved hard work and beatings from my father. But the carpeted aisle and cushioned seats of that aircraft became the setting for a joyous, if brief, holiday for me. I was especially fascinated by the plastic spoons, forks, and knives they gave us with our food. The flight attendants noticed my interest in these utensils, and they started supplying me with some of the extras that were lying around—until I had collected a big bagful! I thought I had really accumulated a treasure, and it took a lot of convincing from my mother to get me to leave them behind and pay attention to my more important baggage.

I guess I was hoping, down deep, that my father's attitude toward the family would change when we moved from one part of the world to another. He did seem in a better mood during the trip. But there were numerous little signs that he was planning to continue his under-the-table dealings in the New World, just as he had in the Old. He swallowed small diamonds and sewed gold coins and other valuables into his clothing so he could slip them by the customs officials. When we finally landed in New York, one of the customs people seemed to smell something in one of our suitcases. As a matter of fact, there were a bunch of cheeses and other foods, which we weren't supposed to be carrying, at the bottom of that case. But there were also some religious icons in the top section of the case, and when my father saw those, his creative mind immediately prompted him to cross himself to distract the official from his search. That was the first and only time I ever saw my father make the sign of the cross.

I lost two of my baby teeth on that flight. I can still remember working on them until they finally came out. What I didn't quite realize, as we left the Port of New York and headed over to catch a flight to Michigan where my oldest brother lived, was that I had lost more of my childhood than a couple of teeth. I was also leaving behind, way back there in Greece, any hope I might have had to retain a little innocence and decency in my life.

As I entered the United States that day, my main goal for the future was rather unusual for a ten-year-old boy. I've told you I wanted to be a priest, and that was still the case. But I also wanted to become a multimillionaire in America, the great "land of opportunity." And then I planned to return to Greece and build a home for all the orphans there. I'm not sure what gave me such a vision at such a young age. Perhaps it was because even though I wasn't an orphan, I felt like one, and my heart went out to many of my friends who had lost their fathers in sea wrecks. I know I felt sorry for them, and I myself knew what it was like to go hungry occasionally. So I wanted to help them, and the best way seemed to be to make a lot of money and go back and build an orphanage home.

Such innocence. I didn't realize that as children grow up and become adults, they face an almost overwhelming temptation to spend their money on themselves and to feather their own nests. And I had no idea what hatred and abuse I was to encounter in the so-called land of opportunity, and how that rejection would work on my mind and reopen the deep, ugly wounds I had suffered as a young boy — wounds that would become so painful that I would lash out mercilessly against others in an effort to relieve my own inner pain.

But I'm getting a little ahead of myself again. As we were waiting in the New York airport for our flight, I was still filled with a sense of wonder at this strange new land. I had never seen a television set in my life, and when I saw some people watching a program in the terminal, I walked over and couldn't believe my eyes. There was this little box with horses running around inside. And there were tiny people riding around on the horses. I wondered how the Americans had shrunk all those people and horses and got them inside that box! We had shadow shows in Greece, where people moved images around in a cardboard box. But that was primitive, like a kind of puppet show — nothing like this television set I was watching.

When we arrived in Michigan, my brother (the war hero) picked us up at the airport and said, "My mule is around the corner here."

We walked out into a parking lot and started looking for an animal tied up among all the motor cars.

But then my brother pointed to a brand new Ford —
his "mule" — and we piled in and headed toward a
house he had rented for us. That was another wonder,
that house. We were used to sleeping seven in a room
in Greece, with everybody on the floor. But now we
had many more rooms, new beds and other furniture,
and even a refrigerator. In Greece, we had also had a
manure pile out behind our house, where we used to
dig for june bugs. I checked behind our new house in
Michigan just to be sure — but, of course, there was
no manure.

My brother owned a restaurant and he gave us all
jobs working for him. I peeled a lot of potatoes and
washed a lot of dishes during the seven months we
spent in Michigan, but I was happy. My big brother
spent about $100 on each of the younger kids for
clothes, and even though I couldn't speak or understand English, I started attending school and got along
as well as could be expected with the American kids
there. At least, the other students left us alone.

But then we moved to Cleveland, and everything
changed. From that time on, things went downhill for
me and the rest of the family. My father did seem to
bring in more money, but as had been the case in
Greece, it never seemed to get into the family coffers.
Instead, much of it went into booze and heavy gambling for my father, and that meant we had to suffer
from his temper during his heavy drinking bouts.

On one occasion, one of my sisters spent six cents
each for about five popsicles which she brought home
to the rest of us kids. Unfortunately, my father walked
in just as we were enjoying the treats, and he flew into
a rage.

"Why do you spend our money on popsicles?" he
shouted. "You want a good time? I'll show you how
to have a good time!"

And with that, he started to beat up on us. He

46

caused such a disturbance that our landlady — who lived downstairs and had been tough on us because she thought we weren't taking good enough care of her wood furniture — threw us out of the house.

The situation that now developed in our family was almost exactly what we had faced back in Greece, before my mother and father separated. We lived in constant fear of a beating and under steady pressure to go out and work so that we could bring in extra income, because my father refused to share much of his earnings with us. Our family situation was worse than it had been in Chios, though, for two reasons: we had no community support and there was no place we could run because neither my mother nor the kids spoke English.

I learned how to pitch pennies with neighborhood kids to pick up a little extra money. I also went into the shoe shine business and found that if I worked hard, I could make a lot of money.

All this may sound like a pretty hard life for a child. But if all I had been confronted with was a bad family environment and the need to work hard to bring in money to help support the others, I think I might have made it all right. The main problem I faced, though, was intolerable pressures at my elementary school. I had gotten along fine with the students and teachers in Michigan, even if we couldn't communicate with each other. But Cleveland was a different story.

The first day I went to my fourth grade class on Cleveland's east side, I got beat up by a bunch of kids for no reason. But frankly, I wasn't so sure whether I had been in a real fight or some kind of rough American game. I had been hit so hard and so often by my father that the blows these kids gave me seemed more like flies buzzing around than any kind of serious brawl. It seemed that these kids were trying to hurt me, because they tore my clothes, but I couldn't be sure — I couldn't understand what they were saying! At any rate, I just kept on walking home until they got tired and left me alone. I had been told by my mom that if I fought or got into any other trouble, the American authorities would do one of two things: ship me back to Greece, or throw me into a dungeon. Since I didn't want to deal with either of those possibilities — and since these kids seemed more a nuisance than a danger — I ignored them.

But it wasn't so easy to ignore my parents when I got home. My mother was the first to see me in my ripped clothes, and she pressed me to tell her what had happened.

"I tripped and fell on the way home from school," I said. That was an easier story than having to explain about those kids.

"You have to keep your eyes open in this country — all ten of them!" she warned. That was an old Greek saying: If you kept your "ten" eyes open, that meant you were being careful.

But while Mom was just content to scold me and then try to help me get cleaned up, Dad was furious, not because I had a few cuts and bruises on my body, but because my clothes had been ruined. So he gave me the *real* beating that the school kids had been unable to inflict.

One of my brothers and I were staying in the same room at that time, and that night, when we went upstairs to go to sleep, I began to pray out loud, as I did every night. I said, "God, help us make friends! We like this country. Help us to win these kids over."

But instead of saying "Amen" to my prayer, my brother muttered, "Let's get some of them. Let's jump on some of those American pigs and get even with them. We can't let them do this to us."

But I kept my eyes closed and continued to pray: "Help us to win them over with love."

"Let's hang or choke a few of them," he responded. "Let's knock some teeth out of their mouths."

I couldn't go along with him — at least not yet. Somehow, as young as I was, I knew it wasn't God's will for me to react with violence.

Mom also wanted to help us settle our differences peaceably with these American kids. She whipped up some tasty homemade cookies and gave them to us to distribute to the other kids in the lunchroom. And we tried her approach as best we could, but with those kids, nothing seemed to work.

Instead of taking our cookies and thanking us for them, they made fun of the big lunches we were bringing to school. Besides all the extra cookies, we carried about five sandwiches each. We were both big eaters, and we couldn't understand these meager one-sandwich lunches the American kids brought. And they couldn't understand us, either — or maybe I should say, they didn't want to understand us. Even though I couldn't catch the words they were using, I could tell by their sneers and gestures that they were making us the butt of their jokes. And once again, they roughed us up before we got home from school.

The final straw, though, was the attitude of our teachers. I think that I might have been able to adjust if some of those teachers in Cleveland had shown some compassion for me. But they were impatient and didn't seem willing to take time to help me learn English better. They taught their classes at a rapid clip, and I couldn't understand a word they were saying. Oh, I caught on to some of the math because arithmetic and numbers are a universal language. But the other subjects were a total loss.

I would watch the teachers closely and try my best to understand them. And when they got way ahead of me, I'd raise my hand to ask a question. But most of them got tired of seeing my hand going up, and they'd send me to the principal's office for disrupting the class too much. It may be that some of the things I did *were* disruptive. I'll give those teachers that much. But I'll tell you this: I certainly wasn't aware I was being disruptive. If I spoke out loud while the teacher was talking, it was just because I was trying to understand what was going on. But this fact never sank in with many of my instructors. So I found myself spending more and more time in the principal's office, often kneeling in a corner as punishment.

I knew I was being treated unfairly. But what could I do? My brother kept urging that we should fight back in some way. But I was reluctant. For one thing, I was a little scared of what might happen if we did retaliate. Also, I really believed things had to change for the better eventually. If we could only hold out until we learned English a little better . . . or until we got a different set of teachers . . . or until God answered my prayers in some way.

But then the roof finally fell in. I still remember that day very well. I should. It was the big turning point for me here in the United States. Pressures had been building steadily. The kids still roughed me up every so often, and my father worked me over much more seriously when I came home with yet another set of clothes ruined.

When I walked into my handwriting class that day, I was tired because I had been out most of the night shining shoes on the Cleveland streets. It was the middle of winter, and I had put some paper in my own shoes to keep the snow from coming in through the holes. I was wearing a pair of blue pants that had been ironed so many times they were as shiny as a mirror. They were certainly clean, though. That was one thing about my mother: she always kept us clean. We might have been poor and been forced to wear old second-hand clothes. But we were scrubbed as clean as you could get. If I said "Good morning!" to my grandmother without washing my face or brushing my teeth, I'd get a slap and a reprimand: "Don't talk to me while you're dirty!"

But my personal hygiene didn't impress the other kids that day. They still made fun of my old clothes. Most days I could have stood their sneers without blinking an eye. That day, though, they started getting to me. I found my seat and sighed with relief when the teacher stood up and started the lesson by having us all sing, "God Bless America." I didn't feel like blessing anybody or anything, especially not America, but at least while we were singing I didn't have to deal with the kids' abuse.

So I joined in the song, even though I still didn't know some parts of it. But as we were singing, the teacher started walking up and down the aisles to see who was singing properly and who wasn't. When she reached me, she stopped and made some remark I couldn't understand when I stumbled over a word. The whole class started laughing, and that was just too much for me. Maybe I should have gritted my teeth and ignored her until she finally let me alone. But that day, I just couldn't. I was a little man. A little Greek man. And my pride had been hurt. I had been made a fool in front of the other kids, and as my anger grew, the hair started standing up on the back of my neck.

So when that teacher laughed at me again, I looked her straight in the eye and laughed loudly and sarcastically right back at her: "Ha! Ha! Ha!"

She looked stunned, as though I had slapped her in the face. The whole class fell silent, and some of the students were looking at me open-mouthed. Nobody had expected the little Greek doormat to respond that way. What was happening?

The teacher recovered quickly though. She grabbed a couple of dictionaries nearby and rapped me over the head with them. I wasn't about to let her get away with that. I pulled those books away from her and slammed her in the face and then in the stomach with them. And I let her have it with my fists, too. I don't know how many times I pushed and kicked her, but when I figured she had had enough, I ran out of the room and down the hall to get my brother, who was in another classroom.

"Let's go home!" I shouted through angry tears. Without asking any questions, he immediately got up and followed me out. He could tell just by looking at me that I meant business, and he was poised and ready. He had been ready for weeks and had just been waiting for me to get pushed over the edge. And that day, I was definitely over the edge, plunging toward a violent fate that most people who knew me later believed could never be altered.

There were extra knives and meat cleavers in our basement, and we headed right down to get them and declared all-out war. I really didn't want to fight. But I couldn't see that I really had any choice. So we packed those weapons around us, in our jackets and down inside our pants, and we hurried right back to school that same day. You can see this wasn't any spur-of-the-moment decision. It had been building for a long time. But now we were like two little volcanoes who, after too much overheating, had finally exploded.

And explode we did. Every kid who had ever stuck out a tongue or made fun of us was marked. I had no love for the American people any more, and especially not for those who had hurt me. We went right up to the kids who had treated us the worst, supposedly the toughest kids in school, and "cocobutted" them in the face with our heads until they were lying bloody on the ground. We grabbed the little girls who had had so much fun at our expense and pulled their hair and punched them.

Our work-toughened little bodies were too much for our softer classmates. We didn't even need our weapons at first. We had them running away from us in all directions, with our flailing bare hands and our coco-butting heads. But then we pulled out our knives and meat cleavers, and a near riot broke out. We were like two little cyclones running loose in that school. Teachers and students alike put as much distance between us and them as they could.

Some school officials finally calmed us down and took us home. And my dad, of course, told us off and beat us up. But I think he was a little bit happy that we had finally fought back. I guess he knew we were starting to be chips off the old block; we were beginning to show our anger the way he did.

For some reason, we didn't get kicked out of school for that incident. We were allowed to return to classes the next day, but this reprieve didn't make us feel any more kindly toward our schoolmates. We were ready for more fighting when we walked onto the school grounds the next morning, and we weren't a bit interested in getting involved in any kind of forgiveness. Many American people, I've learned, are, at the drop of a hat, ready to forgive those who have wronged them. But it's not that way with Greeks. Where I come from, a son might not speak to his father for a lifetime if that father had done something the son considered unforgiveable. The notion of the grudge is well developed among Greeks.

So my brother and I were ready to get down with those kids again and crack some more heads. But we found we didn't have to. Those kids were really afraid of us now. A few of them approached us with money and cookies, either in an effort to buy us off or to make friends with us. It was amazing. We hadn't been able to make any friends when we let them run over us. But now that we had stood up to them, some were too scared not to be friendly. And others who had wanted to be friends but had been reluctant to buck everybody else started to come out of the woodwork and pal around with us. It was the children on the lower end of the social scale who became our buddies, the ones who had been downgraded themselves and now saw us as a way to move up in the school hierarchy.

But now, with our new friends and our growing personal power in that school, we weren't interested in smiling sweetly at our classmates and teachers to gain acceptance. By using violence we had *forced* our enemies to accept us. And even more important than any social acceptance or respect, we found that a little violence applied in the right places could also do wonders to make people give us almost anything we wanted, including their most valued material possessions.

So that's how I began to find my niche in this great land of opportunity. I learned that my own personal America was a land of little or no opportunity, until I finally decided to push aside the usual customs and conventions and take the law into my own hands. I never quite melted into the Great American Melting Pot. I remained an immigrant, a violent stranger in a new and hostile land. And the results were often catastrophic for me and for the lives of the other human beings I touched.

4
The Making of a Mobster

You don't just become a hardened criminal overnight. It takes time. If you asked me to give some instruction on the best way to turn out a professional mobster, my advice might go something like this:

1. Find a young kid who has bad family problems. Look especially for a youngster who's become embittered because he's been rejected flat out by one or both parents. If the child has been the victim of senseless violence in his family, so much the better.

2. Bring this brew of hostility to a boil by thrusting the kid into a social situation where he faces more rejection. You should do your best to put him in a kind of stifling emotional box, where he feels trapped and completely unloved.

3. When he begins to strike back by taking out his hostility on others — and you can bet he *will* take it out on others! — give him a little room to break the law (and other people's heads). Don't impose either tough punishment *or* long-term, loving guidance at this point. Stern discipline or great compassion or some

combination of the two might put the kid back on a law-abiding track again.

4. Sit back and watch him get deeper and deeper into the criminal life. Given a little time, he'll learn all the violence and underhanded skills he needs to become a proficient, dangerous lawbreaker. And if he manages to survive a few shootouts or elude the law for a few years, he may even become one of the best thieves or killers in the business.

I know this is a good way to make a kid into a mobster because it's the route I took. And don't get me wrong: I'm not trying to lay the blame on anybody else. I know I'm primarily responsible for what I became. But I also know I had some help. There were very few people who encouraged me, even for a short time, to put on the brakes in my slide into the garbage world of crime. In fact, most of the people and situations I encountered as a kid seemed to prod me faster and faster into the life of a mobster.

When I finally learned after that first violent eruption at school that violence works, I felt I had discovered the real America for the first time. But I wasn't a total hard guy at this point. I still had little pockets of softness and concern for others in me that had to be rooted out.

The thoroughly cruel, low-down meanness came gradually. But the desire to get power over others swept me along much more quickly, and I learned to enjoy it and use it almost immediately. What kid in my position wouldn't? In a matter of a couple of days, I had soared from the bottom of my school's pecking order to the top. That was heady stuff. I was like a kid with a blank check who had been turned loose in a candy store.

I'm a natural organizer. I have been since I was a

little kid, since those days in Greece when I got the neighborhood children to help me put together funeral ceremonies for dead animals. So it was inevitable that I should see the potential in all those downgraded kids at my Cleveland elementary school who were now looking to me for guidance. They wanted some leadership, and I certainly wasn't about to disappoint them!

It was all sort of informal at first, not really a full-fledged gang in the sense you might understand that word. I would just go to school each morning, and the dozen or so boys who had come to admire me would flock around, waiting for me to tell them what to do. I'd take them out for a walk along the street, and when we came to a parked car, I would point to some cigarettes lying on the dashboard. One of the guys would then break in and get them for me. It was as easy as that.

But then this schoolyard stuff got boring, and we started looking for bigger game. I'd get a bunch of my troops together at night and start doing some more serious stealing. I don't know how many churches we broke into so that we could help ourselves to the poor boxes and other valuables. I also liked to get drunk on the wine the priests kept around for Communion. You can see that by this time, religion didn't mean so much to me any more. I had turned my back on God because I thought I could do better without him. During those late-night forays, we also stole hubcaps, fenders, and other parts of cars that we would then sell to junk yards or to a fence in Cleveland.

I was an especially effective criminal, despite my young age, because I had this burning hatred within me — a hatred that gave me an extra, almost supernatural strength. It was easy for me to hate, not only because I resented the other kids and teachers who had mistreated me, but also because my father's treatment of the family seemed to get worse as the years wore on.

I found myself becoming two different kinds of kids at home and on the outside. I was a kind of Greek Jekyll and Hyde. At home, I was nice and obedient because I thought my mother deserved some respect, and also because I was deathly afraid of crossing my father. I wore old clothes around the house and made a big show of giving him all the money I had in my pocket every day when I returned from work.

But I was a completely different kid the minute I walked out of the front door. I kept a whole wardrobe of expensive clothes at a friend's house, and I'd go over there and change before I went out anywhere with my gang. I could afford some nice outfits because I made a lot of money with my shoe-shining business in local bars. But my income didn't depend only on taking care of other people's footwear. I learned to watch drunks at bars very closely because sometimes, when they'd had too much booze, they'd put their paper money on top of the bar and then forget about it if they got to talking to someone beside them. I'd blow on those loose bills and then pick them up when they floated to the floor. It was finder's keepers as far as I was concerned.

Prostitutes also came over to get me to shine their shoes, and they gave me extra money for directing men to them for their business. Some days, I'd make several hundred dollars from this extra "free-lance" work. Do you know what it's like to be an eleven-year-old kid with a couple hundred bucks in your pocket? It's power and prestige — that's what it is. I was the only guy in my class who wore a $300 ring, and in my own little mind, that put me several cuts above everybody else.

But sometimes I made mistakes, as I tried to keep my home life and my "business" life separate. One of the worst slip-ups happened one day when I came home wearing a new pair of shoes. It was Christmas. I had been polishing shoes in a bar, and I was wearing an old pair of loafers that were full of holes. One of my customers saw what bad shape they were in, and I guess he had a big dose of the holiday spirit that day because he started showing some concern for me. I couldn't understand what he was saying because I still didn't speak English very well. Except for the simplest words and phrases, all I knew were a lot of curse words. I often had to go by the expression on a person's face, and I could tell just by the look on this particular guy's face that he wanted to do something nice for me.

Sure enough, he took me to a nearby store and bought me a pair of new boots and socks. That man's generosity really made my day. I even decided that maybe life wasn't as bad as I had always thought. Maybe there really were some good people out there who had just been hiding in the woodwork, and now they were ready to come out and change my luck.

But that was just wishful thinking. When I went home that night and gave my father about $130 that I had earned during the last few days, he didn't even look at the money. He looked down at my shoes. I had a pretty good idea what was coming, but I still took a stab at trying to explain how a customer of mine had bought them for me.

That was a waste of breath. My father interrupted: "Hey, you thief. You crook! You went and spent my money to buy yourself shoes! I teach you!"

And with that he started to beat me up worse than he'd ever done before. He picked up a cane and began to slam me across the back with it so hard I thought I'd pass out. By the time he had finished, I was bleeding all over, and my body was covered with welts and stripes. Mom tried to stop him, but then she got it too.

If I'd been able to go to bed that night, I'd probably have recovered pretty well by the morning. But I had to go out to work again after supper, and you can imagine I wasn't feeling so good. It hurt to walk and move my arms when I was shining shoes, and I guess I must have been moving so slow and careful that it became obvious to the barmaid that something was wrong with me. She happened to be Greek, and she asked me what my problem was, and I explained to her everything that had happened. So she got in touch with the customer who had bought me the shoes, and the two of them took me home to see my parents.

I don't know exactly what was said at that meeting, but I did pick up a few key words here and there. The man got very angry at my mother and at one point shouted, "Police! Police!" And the Greek barmaid said, "Hey, he was *given* those shoes for Christmas. What kind of people are you?"

My dad didn't care. He just shrugged and turned his back on them. But they really got to my mom. She couldn't take it. She broke down and cried right there in front of everybody.

It was then that my fear of my father started to turn into hate. Part of the reason was that I was getting older and I had had a few more years to absorb his irrational abuse and let it fester in my little brain. But also, I had been young enough when I came to the United States to have my attitudes molded by the values of this country. I had become Americanized more than my older brothers and sisters. And American kids just aren't conditioned to put up with senseless violence from a parent.

So my fantasies began to run toward doing violence to my father. Many times I daydreamed about how I would like to kill him. I wanted to kill him slowly, and the tortures I devised for him in my imagination would make any of the current horror movies seem like a Sunday school lesson.

I think my father must have sensed how I felt, but he didn't do a thing to change my feelings toward him. If anything, he seemed to want to aggravate me even more, maybe to show his continuing power over me. I remember many times during this period he made the children walk seven miles to meet him at Central Market because he wanted to save himself the dime it would have cost for us to take a bus. Then, after we had finished shopping, he told us to carry four big bags, two in each arm, back home another seven miles. Here I was, a leader of gangs who earned my own money and who paid my own bills and many of those of the family, and he was forcing me to waste my time and demean myself this way. And it certainly wasn't that any of us lacked the money for a couple of bus rides. I knew our father would throw away $50 to $100 on a tip at his favorite Greek restaurant when he was in a generous mood.

The cane seemed to keep coming out more often, too. He beat me another time so bad that my wounds bled through my clothes and stained the outside of the back of my shirt. The teachers at school got so upset they called the police to take me home.

It couldn't go on much longer. Everybody in the family sensed that. The incident that finally brought everything to a head happened on one especially bad day, when my father had been abusive toward my mother. The whole situation was working on my mind, and I got madder and madder as I thought about it in bed that night. Who was this man, that he could terrorize an entire household this way? He had no right to push everybody around like this and injure anybody, including my beloved mother, whenever he chose. I worked myself into such a state that I temporarily lost control of my reason. I became an animal in my home that night, the same way I could become an animal on the outside, with my gang. I reached into my drawer, pulled out a knife, and started heading down the stairs toward my father's bedroom.

I guess the creaking of my footsteps on the stairs is what alerted my mother. She came out in her bathrobe and caught me with knife in hand. But even though she stopped me that night, she knew she might not be able to another time. I might make it all the way down to his bedroom, and then what?

She knew we were heading pell-mell for some sort of tragedy, so she decided to take matters in her own hands. She had separated from my father once before, in Greece, and now the time had come for her to do it again. So she and my father got a divorce, and now, finally, for the first time ever, there was the prospect of permanent peace in our home.

But it was too late for me. Sure, it was nice to be able to come home and relax, without any abuse from my father. But my path on the outside had been set. I got deeper and deeper into my gang activities. People were always coming to our home to complain about the things I was doing to disrupt the community. Parents would complain to my mother that I was beating up their sons and daughters. They asked for money to cover the destruction I and my gang had done to their cars and homes. When you saw anybody who looked angry or who had a policeman in tow walking down our street, you could almost always be sure they were heading toward our house. But I would always get even with those who complained. Even the police were afraid of me. Some of them lived in our neighborhood, and they didn't want to get involved with me for fear I'd take it out on their children.

I was thrown out of school regularly for fighting,

and I wasn't even trying to listen to my teachers any more. They had thought at the very first I was trying to disrupt their classes, and they had been wrong. But now, they were right. Dead right. Sometimes I even brought rats to class and set them on fire when the teachers weren't looking — and sometimes when they *were* looking. I wasn't afraid of them or anybody else.

I was finally thrown out of my regular elementary school, and they put me in a special school so I could get some more discipline and also learn to read English better. I was doing seventh grade-level arithmetic, but I couldn't even read the first-grade "Dick and Jane" books.

My experience in that special school almost saved me. And the main reason was a teacher named Mrs. Flanders, the first American teacher I'd ever had who showed me love and understanding.

She won me over the very first day when she found I was a shoe-shine boy, and she said, "Nick, I'd really like to see how you operate. Why don't you bring your shoe-shine box to school tomorrow and show me?"

You can bet that was the first thing I put out to take to school the next morning. I popped my rag for her and really felt proud when she seemed impressed by my style and skill. From that day on, I never missed a day of classes in that school. Mrs. Flanders treated me better than my own Greek people — she even succeeded in getting me to read a little bit. Looking back on the experience, I can even say that I loved Mrs. Flanders. That's how much she meant to me.

And I became something special to her too. She and her husband took me to my very first baseball game, and they also took me on a trip to the Cleveland zoo. I'd never done anything like that before, and I could feel something inside me shifting. I actually started to want to try to establish a good name for myself because I could see there were some rewards in being a nice kid.

But then Mrs. Flanders got sick. Very sick. She missed many classes, and I missed her. I got the bad news one day while I was sitting in her class listening to a substitute teacher. She had died on an operating table. I don't know what was wrong with her. But I do know the impact she had on my life. I cried and cried that day. Tough little Nick the Greek, the gang leader actually shed tears — and over a teacher! A week or so later, I graduated from the sixth grade, and I left all my childhood tears behind, in Mrs. Flanders' classroom.

The next year, I entered a school named Addison. I really hoped I could find a teacher like Mrs. Flanders, or at least a class where I could enjoy some of the schoolwork without having other kids trying to push me around to test just how tough I was. But that wasn't to be. My reputation had preceded me, and I quickly found I had to live up to it.

It happened the very first day I attended classes. I went to the lunchroom, finished my meal, and then walked over to stand in line for a short movie clip they provided for the kids before classes started. A few seconds after I had got in this line, a big kid, a couple of years older, came up to me and said, "I'm going to turn around, and by the time I turn back, there had better be a quarter on the ground for me to pick up."

I looked at him, saw his muscles, and when he turned around, I made sure there was a quarter for him on the ground. But I wasn't about to let things end there. I got a blade and brass knuckles, and I was ready for action.

When I returned to school the next day, I went through the same routine — lunch and the movie line. And once again, this same guy came up to me and said, "I'm going to turn around. And when I turn around, I'd better find a quarter on the ground."

So he turned around. But he didn't turn around again. I had the brass knuckles ready and caught him right on the back of his head, at the base of his skull. I was trying to take half his head off, and he went down, knocked out like a light. Then I took out my blade and like the craftsman I was, I started cutting his pockets and clothes to shreds right on him. I even sliced his shoes apart. That was the beginning of the warfare again. I started coming to school with knives and meat cleavers. Because I knew I wasn't as tough as some guys, I always made sure I had some "equalizers."

As far as school was concerned, I didn't learn much after that. The one course I kind of liked was science. I was fascinated by the section on biology, such as the parts of the eye, like the iris and the cornea. I loved that. But then my science teacher got beat up, and the school officials said I did it—even though I didn't. Then they started pressuring me to snitch on the guy who had done it, but I refused, and that was the end of my science education.

From then on, I spent most of my time fighting or planning fights at school. I organized my gang into subdivisions with names like "Werewolves," the "Greek Spartans" and the "Lone Wolves." One of the groups was best at stealing from cars; another included the best fighters; and each of the others had their own specialties. I even assigned little girls in the school to carry stilettos so they could strike unexpectedly if the boys got into trouble in a brawl.

While kids in other, more civilized schools might concentrate on getting ready for a sports event against some rival school each week, we got our kicks out of staging regular battles with other gangs. I remember one big war we had where I joined forces with another kid who worked for a bakery at the time and had access to some vans, and we planned it so he would arrive with his people in those vans just as the fight started. It was like a major military operation. Just as we confronted that enemy gang, my partner and his boys drove up and piled out with lead pipes, baseball bats, and even a few zip guns. We won that battle easily, but I managed to get hurt bad. I got into a face-off with another guy in a knife fight, and he cut a piece out of my leg before he turned and ran away with his friends.

Kids began to come to me from other schools to beg me to fight for them. Sometimes their problem was that another gang had taken over their neighborhood, and they wanted to get rid of them. So they hired me as an outside mercenary to clean up their area for them. And they paid me anything I wanted — money, sex, booze, jewelry. With one dime in a telephone, I could start a chain of phone calls that would bring out dozens, and sometimes hundreds, of little soldiers who were ready to follow me onto the streets without a moment's hesitation.

I got kicked out of several schools for fighting, and no matter where I ended up, it seemed I always had to confront some guy who wanted to prove how tough he was by challenging me to a brawl. My reputation always seemed to precede me. Things finally came to a head at this one school where, on my first day of classes, the toughest kid and his gang challenged me to a fight.

Of course, I wasn't about to back down. But because I didn't have a gang of my own yet at that school, I found I had to rely on weapons instead of warm bodies to back me up. So I took to carrying a little gym bag filled with ball bearings, knives, meat cleavers, chains, straight razors, brass knuckles, and even a pistol.

I think my enemies at that school didn't really think I'd use those weapons, so they kept testing me, just to see how far I'd go. One of the guys, named Jerry, walked over and sat down beside me in a music class and pulled out a big ball bearing he was carrying in his pocket.

"Hey, Greek, this can really hurt someone," he whispered to me.

"Yeah, and me and my six brothers can do a lot of hurting too!" I said, and I reached into my gym bag for the pistol, which was loaded with six bullets.

"He's got a gun!" Jerry screamed, and he started running toward the door.

That started a stampede out of the classroom, and I decided I might as well help things along, so I fired a round up into the ceiling. I think that whole wing of the school emptied in a matter of seconds.

Sometimes, I think I must have been living in a dream world during that part of my life. I just assumed that our section of Cleveland was the Wild West, and I was perfectly free to walk anywhere I liked with whatever weapons I chose to carry. So I didn't make any changes in my battle gear the next day. I returned to school wearing my leather coat and a stetson, and tugging my gym bag with the knives and pistol in it. I was late getting to my homeroom, and I guess I should have known something was wrong because as I neared the door, I could see all the kids sitting very quietly, looking at me through the door. As soon as I walked into the room, two policemen jumped me and knocked me flat on the floor. When they dragged me outside the building, I was amazed at how many squad cars had lined up around the school — just to be sure I was captured.

They took me to a police station that had a lot of the cops whose shoes I used to shine. One of the policemen, who had been sort of a friend, said, "What have you done, Nick? You got the whole city up in arms!''

They had to throw me in jail, but they didn't want to put me in with the hardened male criminals. They knew that since I was only thirteen or fourteen at the time those guys might molest me. So they put me on the women's side until they could transfer me to a detention home for juvenile delinquents.

Mr. Sampson, one of the head guards there called the other juvenile inmates together the day I arrived and he stood me up in front of them. ''This guy is a snake. Don't double-cross him, or he'll back-stab you.''

So my reputation was made without my having to lift a finger. That night, four of the other inmates woke me up from my sleep and said, ''Hey, man whatever you want to do here, we're with you!''

For a guy like me, that was a golden opportunity — a ready-made gang that was prepared to create havoc at my command. I decided that for my premiere performance at the center I'd start a riot on the first day.

At lunchtime, when one of the wardens said, ''Let's pray,'' everybody else stood and bowed their heads. But I started darting around to the other guys' plates and swiping the meatloaf off them. I stuffed as much of it in my mouth as I could before the prayer had ended, and one of the young inmates finally decided I had gone a little too far for his taste. He was a rough kid himself, and when I reached for the food on his plate, he hit me right in the stomach. All the food I had crammed into my mouth came out all over his face, and that caused the whole situation to explode. Guys started throwing their food around and slugging each other, and I hopped up on the top of my table and began to bust people in the face whenever they got near me.

I lasted only a day and a half in that juvenile detention center. For some reason, though, I didn't get sent to another detention center. The police just took me home until my court date came around. When I finally went before the judge, he had a lot of sympathy for me because I was so young and so he put me on probation.

I never could quite figure out how the criminal justice system worked, but I wasn't about to argue when they let me go. Over a period of time, I came to ignore the whole law enforcement set-up because it didn't scare me a bit. I had learned that despite all the threats of long jail terms they talked about, there was nothing to those threats in practice. I could always work my way out of a jail term, one way or another. The only thing I ever respected was people or organizations that had the will and power to carry through on what they said they were going to do. The cops would sometimes rough me up out on the streets, and I learned to have a healthy respect for them — at least in those cases where I couldn't buy them off. But the courts and judges and jails were nothing to me. They had given me no reason to fear them, so why should I?

So after that little interruption in my gang activity, I went right back to stealing, fighting, and burning houses down. I got my scars from all this violence, too. My whole left eye got pushed halfway out of the socket in one fight, and when I had it checked by an optometrist, he said that with a little more pressure, I would have lost my entire eye.

Soon after this, I quit going to school because I didn't see any point in it. I wasn't learning anything, I was getting into fights I hadn't even been looking for, and I was wasting time I could be using to fine-tune my criminal activity in the community.

So I started leaving home at the usual time in the morning, kissing my mother goodbye, and telling her I'd be home as soon as classes were over. But instead of going to school, I'd meet my gang members and go out and steal cars. We'd find cars parked outside bars and other stores, put them in neutral and push them several blocks away to an old abandoned fire station or vacant lot or some other secluded spot. Then we'd disassemble them and sell the parts to junkyards around the city.

I'd return home late in the afternoon, dirty and greasy, and I'd explain to my mother I was learning to be a mechanic at the shop class at school. She believed me for a while, and I think she was really proud of me when I'd come home, give her some money from what I called my "after-school work," and say, "God bless you, Mom."

I was making several hundred dollars a week at the time from the car thefts, and I could afford to be generous. There was plenty left over to pay for cars for myself and nice girls and entertainment. Mom would sometimes hesitate a little when I gave her the money, and she'd say, "Nick, I don't want any dishonest money or blood money in this house."

But I'd always assure her that I'd earned the money fair and square, and she believed me. But then one day I strolled into the house after a hard day's work of stripping down stolen cars, and she stopped sweeping the floor and asked, "How was school today, son?"

"Fine, Mom, fine," I said.

And with that she hit me with her broom as hard as she could right over the head. And she didn't stop with one blow, either. She started running around the room after me, and I cried, "What's wrong, Mom?"

"I'll teach you to skip school and tell lies to your mother! The police come to my house and you disgrace me. . . . I'll kill you!"

As it happened, a truant officer had been by the house that day asking about me, and he told my mother I hadn't been to classes in weeks. By this time my American-born sister, Diane, was old enough to translate, and she had told Mom what the school authorities were saying. Mom had some reason to be upset, I suppose, but now I was faced with a choice. My brother was already serving time in a boys' detention school, much worse than the one I had been in, and now they were threatening to do the same with me. I certainly didn't want any part of that, so I decided right then and there to run away.

That was a big decision for a fourteen-year-old kid — even one with the rough, independent background I had. I had done some pretty bad things in my life so far, but I still saw myself as a kid in my mother's household. Now I'd pushed her to the limit, and she refused to put up with me any more — and I didn't blame her. You can go just so far in being understanding and lending a helping hand, even with your own children, your own flesh and blood. When they degenerate below a certain point, you have to step back and wash your hands. You can't protect them any longer. And I guess that's the point my mom felt she had reached with me.

Now, for the first time in my life, I was entirely on my own, without any parents to answer to. As I stood hitchhiking on the side of the highway, shivering in an old pea coat as snow and rain fell around me, I sensed I was moving into a new phase in my life, and I wasn't so sure I liked it. But the die had been cast. Despite my youth, I had all the makings of a seasoned criminal. And unless some genuine miracle intervened, I seemed headed directly for a life — and death — in crime.

5

A Search for Freedom

Every kid reaches a point where he cuts his ties with his home and sets out on his own, to find his special little niche in life. I was no exception. The only unusual thing about me was that the home life I was leaving wasn't a secure situation I had to break away from to assert my independence. I *was* independent. I *had* been independent for years. Except for my mother's futile efforts to keep me on the straight and narrow, I had been provided with no honest direction in life. The only thing I had learned at home was that violence, deception, and dishonesty paid off.

But despite the fact that I'd been pretty much my own little man for years, I still had had a warm bed to come home to and a table that my mother filled regularly with food, as best she could. Now, even that little bit of security and stability was gone. My last anchor had been raised, and I was afloat on the storm-tossed seas of the adult world.

But I wasn't free. I figure a Greek on a sea can only be free if he has a rudder and a skilled captain who knows how to use it, a captain who understands how to navigate from one port to another, no matter how rough the water gets. But I didn't have any sense of direction at all as I stood out on that cold highway, waiting for a car to stop and pick me up. I just knew I had to get away from home or take a chance on being imprisoned like my brother. And even though I was a gambler, that wasn't a bet I wanted to take.

Right then, freedom for me seemed like the open road. And West Virginia. That's where I decided to head — West Virginia. Why? I don't know exactly. Maybe I figured that since it was south of Ohio, it would be warmer. *Anything* would be warmer than that highway. Also, West Virginia struck me as being sort of rural, and I needed to get out of the city into the open air. I needed to clear my head and lungs of the atmosphere I'd been breathing in Cleveland and find some time to think.

So after a couple of days on the road, I ended up in West Virginia, at the ripe old age of fourteen-and-a-half. I lied about my age — said I was eighteen — and got a job at a stable brushing and walking horses. But after trying that for a few months, I realized I wasn't cut out for the farm life. The fresh air was great and the pay wasn't bad. But I was a city boy, and there just wasn't enough action in the country town where I had settled. Also, I was homesick. I really wanted to see my mother. One time I tried to call her, just to tell her I was still alive. But when she answered the phone, I hung up without saying anything. I guess I was afraid of what she might say to me — or afraid I might cry or something. I played the part of the big tough guy, and I had knifed and stolen from plenty of people in my day. But down deep, I think I still knew I was just a little kid. My mother was the only person in the world I loved, and I wanted to reach out to her. But I just didn't know how.

I started wanting desperately to go home, but

somehow I just couldn't bring myself to do it yet. So I did the next best thing—I went part of the way to Cleveland and ended up in Akron, Ohio, for a while. I almost had my life completely turned around in Akron, and if I had stayed there a little longer than a few months, I might have been remade into an honest, law-abiding teenager. And if that had happened, the man most responsible for the change would have been a preacher named Raymond Caldwell. I spent some time working and getting into trouble in Akron before I met Rev. Caldwell. As a matter of fact, I had already started to form a gang and was getting my kicks by stealing cars and either stripping them down, or just shoving them off into the Ohio River.

But then some friends invited me to attend a music program at Caldwell's church, and I decided what could I lose? There might even be some good-looking girls there. So I went. And there *were* some pretty girls, a couple of teenagers who sang like angels— and they were both Rev. Caldwell's daughters. One thing led to another, and I managed to meet them and get invited to their family's home for lunch.

I realized right off that I wasn't going to get anywhere in the back seat of my car with these girls, but I soon forgot about trying to seduce them. Rev. Caldwell was the one who had my attention now. I had been impressed with the authority of his preaching, the clear conviction he had about God, and about what was right and wrong. Most of the other ministers and priests I had run into were either too wishy-washy in their beliefs, or just plain hypocritical. I couldn't forget one minister I had stayed with for a while in my travels who couldn't seem to get his doctrines or his morals straight. I'd hear him say, "Well, I know the Bible says Jesus was born of a virgin, but that's not necessarily true. . . ."

And I'd think, "Just who are you to say it's true or

not true? It's not up to you! It's up to the church or the Bible or God or somebody who has more authority than you have!" But I didn't say anything out loud because he was feeding me, and I didn't really care to argue about religion at that point.

So this was the impression I had of the clergy. I decided, "This guy is a lie, and so his God is a lie!"

But Rev. Caldwell made me rethink my position. When he'd get wound up in the pulpit, his eyebrows would arch up and he'd start barking out biblical commands with such authority that I imagined I could almost see fire coming out of his nostrils.

He actually frightened me while I was sitting in the pew listening to him, and I began to toy with the idea that maybe I should consider changing my way of living. But the thing that got to me most, even more than his hell-fire sermons, was the love that he and his family showed me. I thought my mother was the only person in the world capable of showing real love, but the Caldwells proved me wrong. I did some odd jobs for their church, like painting one of the buildings and stripping off some wallpaper, and they took me right into their family activities. Caldwell showed me a lot of the little warm, family touches that I'd never known before — like how to make ice cream out of snow. I'd never thought of that, but it sure seemed to be a lot of fun.

Rev. Caldwell knew I wasn't a very religious person. In fact, he may have suspected I was actually a pretty bad person. I wouldn't be surprised if he had figured me out pretty well because I know how hard it is to hide your real nature from another person you're in close contact with over several weeks. I imagine he'd heard something about those cars I'd pushed in the river. I had never been caught by the police, but rumors start floating around when you're flirting with the garbage world, and I'm sure there were plenty of rumors in Akron about me.

But despite what he might have heard or known, he accepted me. And I respected him and became almost fanatically devoted to him because of that. But he kept on after me about Jesus, and I wasn't ready to get involved with any serious religious stuff just yet.

He'd say, "Nick, don't you think you ought to consider Jesus? Don't you want to accept him as your Savior?"

But I'd just make a joke or change the subject. I liked Caldwell too much to hurt his feelings by telling him to get off my back, but I wasn't about to commit my life to this guy's God at this point. My God was still Greek — if he existed at all. I was willing to concede that Rev. Caldwell had an impressive faith, one that was consistent and had turned him into a wonderful person, one of the best I had ever met. But this Jesus wasn't for me.

What *was* for me was some regular female companionship, and so my mind started drifting to an old girlfriend named Sharon I had left behind in Cleveland. I had had a big dose of God and religious living, and now I was ready for something evil. There were ingrained habits in my personality, deeply-dug grooves that I always seemed to stumble into eventually, no matter how long I might walk along their ridges, on higher ground. I wanted the worldly glitter and I wanted the power I had wielded on the streets of Cleveland. That had been nearly two years ago, and I was now sixteen, though I still passed myself off as eighteen. It didn't occur to me that maybe time had erased some of the bad memories of the pain and rejection and filth I had encountered as a youthful criminal in Cleveland. No, I looked back on those days as a kind of golden age when I had exercised a lot more freedom in getting pleasure and power than I now had.

So I pocketed the $3,400 I had saved while I'd been away, packed my new suits of clothes, and headed for Cleveland again, this time to return home the conquering hero and rise to even greater heights — or lower depths — than ever before.

I had expected to spend some time in Cleveland when I returned. Maybe even settle down there for good. But things didn't work out that way. One problem was that nobody in my family liked the idea of my getting involved again with Sharon. My brother started going out with her to show me she wasn't just waiting around for me. My mother didn't want me involved because Sharon wasn't Greek. And *her* father wasn't so crazy about me, either.

But I guess everyone likes to think he has someone special, and, most important, she was *willing* to run away with me. She was lonely and confused herself, so we fulfilled some of each other's needs. Even though I didn't fully grasp this at the time, what I really needed was someone whom I could open up to, someone who would respond in a loving way to me. Other than Mrs. Flanders, I never had a teacher who took an interest in me as a person. My classmates either made fun of me or feared me, so I couldn't talk to them. I never had a father I could tell my heart to. To this day, it's hard for me to open up to people. And in those days, *nobody* could get inside Nick Pirovolos. I only let people know what I wanted them to know. There were high, thick walls around my heart. I had learned not to trust anybody.

But even with all my inner walls and mistrust, I decided someone was better than no one. So this girl became my possession, just like my gun or the "leathers" I wore. The fact that my family was against our relationship also drove me closer to her. I just had to show them that I ran my own life. Finally, when I decided I had had enough of being hassled, we hit the open road.

At this stage of my life, I had developed a personal philosophy which was not particularly praiseworthy. But it had served me fairly well in helping me not only survive, but also sometimes even thrive in the shady situations in which I often found myself. There were two basic tenets to this world view I'd come to accept.

The first came from some old Greek song: "Live while you can!" I decided that life was too short to waste time on long-term goals or abstract notions of good and beauty that I couldn't touch, taste, or feel right now.

The second was my own version of the Golden Rule: "Do unto others before they do it unto you!" It didn't matter if you had to cheat, steal, or kill to get the upper hand over other people. The important thing was just to *get* the upper hand.

Those were the main principles in my personal religion in those days — not too profound, maybe, but they seemed to work quite well for me. Of course, I had no idea where such convictions were leading me in the long run. I wasn't at all interested in the long run! I only wanted to know about the here and now. How can I increase my pleasure and contentment this instant? I had completely forgotten other principles, such as the *constructive* Greek sayings my mother had taught me — sayings like "Show me your friends, and I'll tell you who you are." I never considered that my friends and companions might provide a mirror image of who I was and what I was becoming. If I had looked closely at these people I was associating with, I would have seen a bunch of social misfits, losers who had been unable to make it in the legitimate world and had turned to crime and prostitution to try to make up for their inadequacies.

But I didn't have time to think about things like that. I was a man of action, an adventurer, a hero out of the mold of Ulysses—or so I thought. The armchair philosophers and weaklings could sit around and muse about the meaning of life. But as for me, I was going to take a big bite out of life before it took an even bigger bite out of me. I wanted total freedom, and the open road seemed the answer to my quest.

So Sharon and I, two kids in their mid-teens who weren't even old enough to qualify for an adult I.D. card in any state, set out to conquer the country. First, we went to Detroit, Michigan, where we worked up a con game to get money from guys coming out of bars. Sharon fixed me up with a mustache and a beauty mole so I'd look like a soft pushover, and then she played like a hooker. She would lure a guy over into an alley after he came out of the bar, and then I'd walk over, pull out a gun or machete, and work him over until he gave us all his money.

But then things got too hot in Detroit for us because the police and bar owners caught onto our game, so we hit the road again, and this time ended up in Wisconsin. Don't ask me why Wisconsin. We just hitch-hiked until we got tired of riding, and then we stopped for a while. But it wasn't a very long stop. The cops there soon got after us for shoplifting and some illegal gang activity, and before we knew it, we were on the road again, this time heading for Georgia.

Why Georgia? Again, I don't know. I guess I thought there might be some adventure, some "business" opportunities, some real freedom down there. But I didn't dwell too much on heavy, global thoughts. I mainly just lived for the pleasure of each day and let tomorrow take care of itself.

The only problem was that there wasn't much pleasure those days we were heading toward Georgia. Not many people picked us up, and so we often found ourselves walking whole days and nights just to get a few miles closer to our destination. And those who *did* pick us up were often dangerous. We were both obviously young, and some drivers got it into their heads that it might be fun to take advantage of us. The main thing most of them were interested in was getting rid of me and taking Sharon off somewhere and making out with her. But I always carried one of my "equalizers" — such as a thin, easily concealed linoleum knife that got us out of more than one scrape.

Finally, we did make it to Atlanta in one piece, mainly because we lucked out and got a ride from a nice truck driver who wasn't obsessed with seducing Sharon. I think he saw us for what we were — a couple of pitiful kids who were wandering around aimlessly and bound for some kind of big trouble if we didn't put down some roots in a decent place. So he took us under his wing and even got me a job in a dog food factory when we arrived in Atlanta.

The pay was good enough that I was able to save some during the few months I worked there. But I wasn't cut out for honest work. I knew that. Even though I could make a fairly good living as a laborer, I knew I could make a lot more — and have a lot more excitement — if I returned to the world of crime. So I started hanging around with the loafers and petty criminals in some of the local bars. One thing led to another, and I ended up losing my job.

That was when I decided to get into mind reading. One of my relatives, the one who had been into witchcraft back in Greece, had been on my mind during this trip. Even though I had feared her as a child, I now began to think she and I might have a lot more in common than I had first realized. I also remembered what a wandering gypsy had told me when I was a kid, about how my eyes had a special power in them.

"God help women from your eyes!" he had said. "God help people away from your eyes. You're going to destroy lives or be a great man—just because of your eyes."

He might have been right, I decided. In any case, it couldn't hurt to see if I had inherited some of the occult powers that my relative possessed. I had rejected God by now and was already looking at myself as a relative of Satan. So why not take advantage of some of the devil's demonic powers to better my station in life?

So I set up a fortune-telling room right in my home, put on a turban, and called myself Magi. And to my surprise, people started taking me seriously and coming in to seek out my advice. It wasn't that I really thought I could tell people what their future would hold. But I did think I had the power to exercise a certain control over human beings—a control that would enable me to get some money out of them. For example, one woman who came in to see me was quite upset because her boyfriend had been in a terrible accident, and she was very concerned about what the future held for him and her relationship with him.

I was enough of a con man that I knew how to say just enough to her without getting so specific that she would know I was a phony. I had learned early in this new game that it was best to throw out something vague and then let my "clients" fill in the information I didn't know. More often than not, they could be tricked into believing that I knew more than I really did because, without realizing it, they were supplying me with facts about themselves I could never have discovered otherwise.

"I see three . . . I see three . . . what does that mean?" I said to the woman.

"Well, my boyfriend has three sons!" she exclaimed, as though I had popped up with some deep secret about the fellow. And now I knew from the way she had answered the question that her lover had probably been married before or at least had been the father of three kids before he got involved with her.

So now I said, "I see two women going for this man."

"Oh, yes, that's me and his wife!" she said, once again shocked at how much I knew about her.

"And now I see the number five," I said.

But before I could get another word out, she interrupted, "There are five doctors working on him!"

And so on we went, with me throwing out meaningless facts and with her filling in all the blanks so that quite soon I had a complete picture of the woman, her boyfriend and their relationship. I often ended up saying something like, "You're going to get a phone call when you get back home. It will ring soon after you return and will have important meaning for you in the future."

That was a pretty safe prediction since almost *everybody* gets phone calls periodically during the day. And the chances were also pretty good that this woman would get an important call since her boyfriend was lying in a hospital bed and she was probably on the phone constantly, talking with her friends and relatives about his condition.

I can't count the times I gave people advice about how to lead their lives—and amazingly, they often took it. And it was all phony. I played into their unspoken fantasies and desires and placed prophecies in their minds that I'm sure, in some cases, became self-fulfilling predictions. In other words, some people so desperately wanted the future to turn out as I had predicted that they lived their lives in ways that made my prophecies come true.

I sensed I was dabbling in a very evil area, but I didn't care. In fact, I prayed to Satan, "Give me power! I'll serve you any day of the week if you increase my power over others. I want to be your right hand man so that I can have every material thing I dream of and have people doing whatever I ask."

It was about this time that I started calling myself "the devil's son-in-law."

But despite my sworn allegiance to him, the devil didn't lift a finger to keep me from getting kicked out of Macon by some of the solid citizens in my neighborhood. I had taken to drinking heavy and hanging around with the criminal element again, and I'd occasionally shoot up the neighborhood with one of my guns when I'd had too much booze. I actually had to make my final getaway with a cocked shotgun in my lap because some people thought I had done them wrong and they wanted me to pay up or suffer the consequences before I left.

So Sharon and I headed for Florida this time, and I didn't hesitate when I got there to find out how I could enter the Miami crime connection. Legitimate work was beginning to become secondary for me now. If I took a regular job, it was only because I might need an honest front to cover the much bigger money I was making in crime.

I got into the gambling scene very heavily in Florida, and I also worked as a runner for bookies and other criminals who wanted to "launder" their money in legitimate businesses. In other words, they would make their money illegally in some sort of criminal activity, and then they would use me to take it over to a "laundromat," or legitimate business. The illegal money would be absorbed into the legitimate income and ledgers of the honest business, and this would make it hard for the cops to trace the source of the criminal income.

But I was too young and too wild to stay in one

place very long. Even though I was making good money, I spent it as fast as it came into my pocket — and as often as not, I put most of what I earned into fast cars, gasoline, and booze. That combination resulted in so many speeding tickets the Florida police finally put out a warrant for my arrest. They caught me carrying a concealed weapon, but before they could nail me permanently, we took off once again on the open road.

The traveling was getting old now. I had been gone from Cleveland for nearly two years, and even though I'd had some excitement, I couldn't really say I'd had a lot of fun. We stopped off in Akron so I could play the big man around Rev. Caldwell and the other people I knew there. I had some money and I passed Sharon off as my wife. Being a respected man of means in Akron sort of made me feel cockier than I had in a long while, so I decided to hang around there for a few weeks and bask in this unexpected glory a little longer.

I got a job in a restaurant as a cook and I even briefly considered staying honest so my Akron friends would think I was an upstanding citizen. But I couldn't stay out of the criminal world. No matter how hard I tried — and I didn't try very hard — I couldn't reject the glitter and temptation of fooling around on the wrong side of the law. So I started spending more and more time in some of the bars where I knew the criminal families in Akron — the Greek and Italian and Turkish underworld elements — hung out. Soon, some of the "soldiers" from these families were knocking on my door, saying "Come on, Greek, let's talk."

And talk we did — about laundering money, carrying messages for bookies, blackmail, arson, violence. I knew about all those things. I was just a teenager, but I already had a graduate degree in street crime.

My web of contacts had spread out so far that now, no matter what big city I stopped in, I knew somebody who knew somebody. I had references and I had experience. My "resumé," if you want to call it that, was becoming attractive to the big mobsters, and I liked the higher status I was being given in their garbage world. I wasn't just a kid any longer. I sensed I was on the verge of making it big. And I decided my home town, Cleveland, was going to have the honor of being my base of operations for a highly successful career in crime.

6
A Career in Crime

There's an old Greek story about camels in a caravan. It seems that this one camel was walking behind another in single file, and she looked up and all she could see was the other one's hump. The sight cracked her up because she thought she had never seen anything so funny as a hump on a living creature. The thing was, she couldn't turn around and see her *own* hump.

Greeks say people are like that. They look at each other's humps and laugh. But they never bother to take a look to see if they have any humps of their own. I was like that, too, all my life, but especially when I returned to Cleveland after my travels around the country.

I thought I was a little man of the world. I thought I knew all I needed to know about making it big on the seamier side of life. I was sure I understood everything about playing the angles and applying violence to make people and situations march to my beat. I knew I had failed to find the freedom and power and money I had searched for on the road. But that didn't matter to me because I had learned a lot about my chosen profession. I was more aware now of what worked in the underworld and what didn't. And I was convinced that I could eventually make crime pay a lot more handsomely than an honest job in some restaurant or other sweatshop.

But I was blinded to my own shortcomings. I thought I was different from every other petty little hood in town. I also thought I was different from my friends, many of whom ended up in jail.

One of my main things had always been making easy money from fencing hot merchandise or from gambling. I'll have to admit, though, that I wasn't really the best holdup man around. My problem was that I was a pushover for a sad story. The very first man I held up actually ended up with some of *my* money. Some friends of mine and I had staked out this one guy to see what his schedule was as he walked home so we'd know best how to rob him. We finally thought we'd figured the exact spot and time that would be easiest to get him, and I hid near the location with a ski mask over my face.

But for some reason, the victim we'd picked didn't show. Instead, this other old guy finally came along, and I decided I'd stick him up instead, so I wouldn't have to go back empty-handed to the car where my buddies were waiting for me.

So I jumped out in front of this old guy, stuck my pistol in his face, and said, ''Gimme all your money!''

He gave me his wallet all right, but then he started crying. The old guy was actually standing there on that sidewalk in front of me bawling his eyes out! He didn't have a cent in his wallet, and I could tell by looking at him more closely he was sort of down and out. He probably thought I was going to kill him if he didn't give me something. I felt so sorry for him that I reached into my own pocket, pulled out a couple bills, and put them into his wallet. He just stood there staring at me as I walked away. I'm sure he was wondering what kind of strange thieves they had in this part of town.

But even though I got a little soft sometimes, all that softness disappeared whenever I learned somebody was trying to take advantage of whatever was left of my better nature. My partners and I once decided to hit a local hamburger joint, and we went in just as they were closing. I pulled my gun on the man behind the counter.

The guy started to whine, "I just got out of the army, and I've got a wife and children. Don't do this to me! If I lose all this money, I'll lose my job. The manager of this place doesn't have a heart."

"Okay, okay," I said, and I motioned to my guys that we'd let this place go. I sure didn't want to put a poor young family man out on the streets.

But the next morning as I was shaving, I heard on the radio that this man had gone to the police and was bragging about how he had tricked this robber the previous night. It seemed the guy wasn't an employee at all. He was really the manager, and he had told me a bald-faced lie to get me off his back. That's fine. I could take the lie. But if you put one over on me, you don't go around bragging about it. I had a reputation to maintain.

So we returned to the restaurant just as it opened up that day. When the guy saw us walk through that door, all the color drained from his face.

"Open that safe, right now!" I ordered.

"No," he said, but it was obvious he wasn't so sure of himself now.

Then I grabbed his hand, held a meat cleaver over

it, and said, "You're only going to get one chance to open that safe or I swear to you, I'll take off your hand."

And I *would* have taken his hand right off. Make no mistake about that. The manager obviously knew I wasn't fooling, and he also knew that the softness he had seen in me the night before had vanished completely. I was an animal now. An angry animal. And lucky for him and me, he realized it. So he went right to that safe, opened it, and we walked off with every cent he had on hand.

I may not have been the toughest, most natural holdup man in the world. But I liked the money well enough to keep working at it and to try for higher and higher stakes. You could get some decent pocket change by sticking up individuals on the street and knocking over small stores. But I was more ambitious than that. I got to thinking, "Where's the place I'm most likely to get the largest amount of money?" And the answer that came to my mind immediately, of course, was a bank!

Now, I didn't know beans about how to rob a bank. Everything I had heard about bandits going in and holding up tellers in broad daylight during business hours seemed a little too dangerous. And the odds seemed stacked against success. The thieves were always either getting killed or getting caught. And there was the problem with picking up marked money and all the other safeguards banks were supposed to have.

It seemed to me that rather than walk in like Jesse James during the day, it would be smarter to break in at night. I knew something about breaking and entering, and I figured a bank would probably be pretty much the same—especially if you came in through the roof. So I got about six guys together and without much more of a plan than the vague idea that we'd pick up any loose bags of money that were lying around, we went up onto the roof and broke in through a door up there.

We had been inside the building only a few minutes when all of a sudden sparks started to fly around all over the place and an alarm went off. Everybody panicked and started heading toward the nearest windows and exits.

I somehow managed to make it back out onto the street, and as I ran down the sidewalk, I heard somebody yelling, "Stop!" Then there were a couple of loud cracks, and I felt this nudge in my hip. After I had gone several more blocks, I couldn't run another step. There was this burning sensation in my backside, and when I put my hand back there, I felt blood. To cover up any stain on my pants, I took off my jacket and tied it around my waist so that it hung way down on the back of my legs. Then I headed for home real slow. The pain was so bad, I could hardly walk by the time I reached my front door.

My mom was cooking when I passed her in the kitchen, and I tried to put up a good front for her: "Hi, Mom, I'm going to take a bath before supper."

Somehow, I made it up to the upstairs bathroom, and when I got inside, I locked the door and went to work with some crude first aid. I took my sister's mirror, some tweezers and a knife, and I also pulled out a bottle of Aqua Velva aftershave lotion. Then I cut right into my hip and dug down until I found the bullet. It hurt pretty bad. But I could take almost anything if I knew it was only going to hurt one time. I learned how to doctor myself pretty well after this first gunshot wound. But I also learned that if I wanted to stay healthy during my budding crime career, I'd better stay clear of banks.

So I decided to stick with other businesses when I was in the mood for stealing. Of course, you have to be very choosy about the places you hit. You watch them closely, do some research on the times of day when the most money is likely to be inside — and then you strike.

The biggest job I ever put together was also potentially the most dangerous because it involved a bookie joint. In one way, bookie joints are easy pickings for a robber because the chances are pretty good there will always be plenty of money lying around. But in another sense, they're the toughest places to hit because they're always mob-owned. That means you're likely to run into heavily armed guards, guys who know how to shoot a piece and don't hesitate to blow your head off if you look even slightly suspicious. Also, if they find out who you are, you'll never be safe even if you manage to get away with the money.

But I liked excitement, and I was sure I was going to live forever. Also, I was real interested in getting a lot of money as fast as possible so I could live like the big godfather I wanted to be. You put all this together, and a bookie joint was a natural target for me.

My buddies and I picked the biggest place we could find on the outskirts of town. There were five of us on this job, and we charged through the doors wearing ski masks and waving these big pistols at everybody in sight. I had been there many times before and had cased the place pretty well, so I knew the layout. In one corner, a bunch of guys were "wrapping up" the money they had taken in that day and binding it in tens, fifties, and hundreds.

I was feeling real mean. I yelled, "Don't anybody move or I'll shoot!"

This one guy flinched a little and I shot him right in the leg. There wasn't any reason to do that. But like I said, I was feeling mean. With the sound of that shot still echoing in the room, those guys knew we meant business. They knew we were the heavies for the time being, so they cooperated completely. As I saw all that money being poured into the bags we'd brought, I knew we'd struck gold this time.

"Let's split!" I said as soon as we had filled up the bags, and we ran to our car which we had stolen just for this job. We took off so fast that I was pinned against my seat for the first block. Then we reached another car we had hidden a mile or so away from the bookie joint, and I drove the original getaway car with all the money while the other guys took off in the safe car. I was the one who was supposed to dispose of the hot car, and I was happy to drive it. I wanted to be alone for a little while with all that money.

My first stop wasn't the garage where I was going to ditch the stolen car. It was an apple orchard down the road. I pulled the car to a halt and immediately sat down to count our take. There was $129,000 in those bags — enough to live well for a little while, but not as well as I could have if I didn't have to split the loot evenly with my henchmen. So I decided to cheat them. They say there's no honor among thieves, and that's true. I'm living proof. I figured if they were stupid enough to let me get off alone with all that money, that was their problem, not mine.

I quickly counted out about $50,000 for myself, and that left about $20,000 for each of the other guys. Just to make things look right, I left $20,000 of my money in with the main amount so that when it was divided, it would look as though I were getting an equal share. But then I took the remaining $30,000 and buried it there in the orchard where it would be ready for my use later.

The other guys in the gang were a little suspicious when I finally showed up with the bags of money at the place where we had arranged to meet to make the final division. But they didn't know exactly how much we had stolen. And I wasn't about to tell them. I never worked with that gang again. That shows some thieves have got good judgment, I suppose. And if they had known how I'd cheated them, I'm sure they would have been happy to know what finally happened to the extra amount I'd stolen from them. I lost every cent of it in a few hours on the gaming tables in Las Vegas.

I liked to stage armed robberies and other thefts because the money I stole could buy me nice clothes, the finest food in any restaurant, and slick cars which would make most girls look twice when I roared past. But I also liked the violence and excitement. In time, this obsession with using force to wield power over others became a dominant element in my personality. I liked to push people around and inflict pain on them, for no other reason than that it amused me. Force applied strategically to individuals and groups of people could make them respond, like animals in a cage. It gave me a special kind of power over them, and I liked that. Power turned me on as much as money did.

One of the most effective means I found for exercising this kind of violent power (and making money at the same time) fell into my lap by accident. One day I was driving along a country road in Ohio, near the Pennsylvania line, and my tire went flat. As I started working on the tire with my jack, I heard a horse trot up behind me. When I turned around, what should I see but this big dude, high in the saddle, with a rifle strapped to his back. Another guy was galloping up right behind him. They both looked pretty mean — like they didn't like the idea I had decided to have a breakdown where I did. I knew I was at something of a disadvantage, so I just stood up, looked at them as friendly as I knew how, and decided not to speak until I was spoken to.

"Hey LeRoy," the closest horseman yelled back to his buddy, "should we shoot this one?"

I decided I'd better get into this conversation before it went any further. "Hey, man," I said, "I just got a flat tire and I want to fix it and get out of here!"

"Okay, honky, we'll let you go this time," the second horseman answered. "But you get out of here right now and don't come back!"

"It'll just take a second to fix this tire —" I started to say, but the guy interrupted me.

"No, you forget that tire and get out of my sight."

I wasn't about to argue since they had the rifles, so I hopped into the car and drove off down the road with my flat tire flapping and grinding against the wheel rim. Of course, my tire was ruined when I reached the nearest gas station, and I had to fork out a lot of money to get the mechanic to put the wheel back in order. As I was waiting for the repairs to be made, I found a bar and started drinking. And the more I drank, the madder I got.

"Those guys can't do this to Nick the Greek!" I muttered to myself. "They're not going to get away with this."

So as soon as my car was fixed, I headed back toward the spot where I had encountered those horsemen. I didn't know what I was going to do when I got there. I didn't even have a gun on me, and they were armed with high-powered rifles. But when you're drunk, you don't think straight. And when *I* get drunk, I've got the added disadvantage of being half crazy. All I knew was that I was mad and I was going to get them, one way or another. So I kept on driving, past the spot where I'd had the flat, until finally I came to a house in the middle of a pasture. I figured this must belong to those guys because it seemed part of the same fenced-in property.

I roared up to their front door and slid to a stop in a

cloud of dust. Then I got out of my car and slammed the door and waited for them to appear. Like I say, I don't know what I had in mind. If they had come out of that door, I'm sure I'd soon have been a dead man—or at least I'd have spent a few days in the hospital if I could have found my way to a hospital.

But there was nobody home. What now? I looked around, and my eye came to rest on a U-Haul truck not too far away. I walked over and looked through a window on the truck, and what should I see but a full-fledged arsenal. My heart started to pound so hard I could hardly contain myself. There were rifles, handguns, grenades, automatic greasers, an M-60 machine gun, and boxes and boxes of ammunition. For a guy in my chosen field of work, it was like a dental student walking out of his graduation ceremonies and stumbling into a fully equipped office, free of charge!

The car I was driving happened to have a trailer hitch on the back, so I backed it over to the U-Haul, attached my car, and took off down the road, whistling the Greek national anthem. I knew now that I had stumbled onto the weapons cache of some militant group. I had heard they had a farm in this area, and now I was real happy I'd been able to pay them a visit. Nick the Greek always gets the last word, I thought. If those guys had just been nice to me, they'd have been rid of me and still had their weapons—which I was certain were worth tens of thousands of dollars. But they had chosen to fool with the Greek, and they had to pay the price.

As I drove back home, my mind was buzzing with the possibilities now before me. I knew I probably had more firepower now than any other single man in Cleveland—and probably more than any of the individual crime families in the city as well. That made me a power to contend with, but the question was, how could I best use that power and increase my income at the same time?

I knew there was no point in my just hoarding all these weapons and ammunition for myself because I probably wouldn't get into that many shootouts during the rest of my life. I was learning, though, that the essence of being a good leader, whether in a legitimate field or in the garbage world, was to delegate power, and spread your influence among as many people and groups as possible. I decided this was exactly what I would do with these weapons. I would become a mercenary and arms merchant by selling the least valuable guns at bargain prices and then renting out the most valuable weapons, like the big machine gun, to gangs that were interested in warring with other gangs or instigating riots.

My rental rate for the M-60 machine gun was $25 a day if the gun wasn't shot, another $25 if they used it, and an extra $100 if they wanted to hire me to do the shooting. Even if I wasn't hired to participate in the fighting, I sometimes went along as a spectator. I still remember this one gang war where one side had rented my machine gun. I hadn't been hired as a mercenary, but I wanted to watch the show, so I propped myself up on a chair in a nearby gas station and slurped on a can of Budweiser as the two sides started moving toward each other.

It was like the gunfight at the O.K. Corral. Bullets whizzed through the air, and several crashed into the window panes in the gas station just behind me. Everybody else at the station had long since either hit the floor or run away, but I sat right up there in my chair watching everything with a stupid, drunken grin on my face.

I really *enjoyed* watching people fight. Whenever a stray bullet would hit something near me, I'd just yell, "Hey, you missed!"

The police finally showed up and started giving orders through megaphones: "All right, everybody is under arrest!"

But the gunmen just ignored them and kept on shooting at each other. I figured that this must only be the first wave of cops. A full-blown riot squad would arrive before long — and they hadn't even started shooting my machine gun yet!

I wanted more fireworks, more bloodshed, so I yelled, "Hey, you guys, what about the machine gun?"

And almost as if they were acting on my cue, a Chevy roared around the corner with the machine gun blazing out one of the windows. It was the most incredible sight I'd ever seen. It was almost dark, and you could see the colored tracers from the machine-gun bullets flying through the air like a major fireworks display. The only thing was that we weren't dealing with fireworks — this was the real thing. Loose earth and asphalt exploded into the air as the machine-gun rounds hit the ground.

Needless to say, the side I was supporting won. The machine gun had tipped the balance in their favor. I know many people were seriously wounded. But I didn't even think twice about that. All I cared about was that I had made a little money and seen some excitement. That's what life's all about, isn't it? At least, that's the way my mind worked at the time of that shoot-out.

Something was happening to me about this time, something I was only vaguely aware of. I was getting harder inside. Most of the softness and sensitivity I'd had as a kid had disappeared, like the early morning fog on a Greek sea. There was a tough shell around me now.

Also, my life was gradually speeding up, like a movie projector that's gone out of control.

Like I said, I wasn't fully aware of what was happening to me. All I knew was that nothing seemed to satisfy me completely anymore — not my former levels of violence, not my women, not my booze. So I kept trying to cram more and more into each day, and I began to act crazier and crazier. I did things no sane human being would ever do. I suppose if I had stopped for a minute and just thought about what I was doing, I might have regained control over the pace of my life. But I didn't have time to stop. I didn't have time to think. All I had time for was to satisfy whatever craving might overtake me at any given moment.

For a while, I drove a bullet-proof car for one of the "big boys" in Chicago crime, and I had several other underworld assignments that brought in a good bit of money. Of course, I never saved a cent. I lived only for what I could get out of each day. I didn't care who I hurt as long as I did what satisfied me.

Through these connections and my own spirit of free enterprise, I managed to open a gambling hall, staffed with professional dealers and several prostitutes. The cops busted us regularly, and I learned the most efficient ways to pay them off so I could get back on the street and start earning my money again.

The arresting cop might say, "We don't know if we should put you in jail now, or let you go. . . ." And when that hesitation came in his voice, and when I saw that knowing look in his eye, I knew that was my signal to fork over some money. But how much? That was always the question. If I offered too little, they might turn me down or even charge me with bribery, and that sure wouldn't keep me out from behind bars very long. But if I offered too much, I'd be that much further behind in trying to increase my own profit margin.

But I learned. Through trial and error, I learned. I

once had to pay an entire precinct close to $7000 to convince them to let me stay open. It was a lot of money, but it worked. That was heady stuff for a young immigrant boy, who only a few years before had been treated like the scum of the earth by his American classmates. They had called the tune for me in those days. But *I* was calling the tune now for a significant bunch of officials in the high-and-mighty American criminal justice system. It might be costing me 7,000 bucks, but that was a small price to pay to have several dozen cops in my employ, tipping their blue hats and calling me by name when they passed me on the street.

I was an upwardly mobile young mobster, on a fast track to the top. And I should have been happy and contented. But I wasn't. Something was wrong — something inside, down in the deepest wellsprings of my Greek soul. One symptom of the mysterious malady that had infected me was my drinking. I could drink a fifth of scotch in a single night, easy. Then I'd take several cans of beer on top of that as a chaser. I also got into marijuana, cocaine, and other drugs a little. But booze was my main thing because I always wanted to feel in control and feel powerful, and liquor could do that for me. Actually, I usually ended up totally *out* of control after a few drinks. I got into the worst fights and the most danger when I was tanked up. It got to the point where I couldn't go into a bar without getting into a brawl. I was bad enough sober. But liquor turned me into a complete animal.

One of the reasons I did such heavy drinking in those days was that I was having a lot of trouble sleeping. I had to drink myself silly so I could get some sort of night's rest. If I didn't drink enough, my whole body would twitch while I lay there in bed. I'd have nightmares almost as soon as I drifted off —

sometimes I was on my way to hell, or I was falling down, down through this scary black space.

One day, when I had just returned to Cleveland from a drunken binge down in Las Vegas, my mother asked me to come over and paint her house. I went over but I gave her some excuse about being too tired, and I fell right off to sleep on her sofa. I immediately started dreaming about entering this huge castle of a house. It was a beautiful place, with mahogany paneling, and this fat man was showing me around from floor to floor. When we reached the attic, I saw a big, expensive AM-FM radio over in the corner, and I thought, "I'm going to come back here and steal that radio."

Then, as we walked back downstairs, we passed some puppies and I reached over to pet them, but their mother, this big, mean German shepherd, popped up out of nowhere and pounced on me. I started running back up the stairs to get away from her, and I was in such a panic my heart was in my throat. As I ran up and up, I passed a big statue of Jesus, who seemed to be holding out his hands toward me. I thought, "Hey, man, this must be a good dream because Jesus is in it!"

But then the statue of Jesus fell over, and I decided I'd better keep on running. Finally, I reached the top and saw this beautiful woman on a ledge just above me. She had the most stunning, long hair I'd ever seen, and she reached down toward me with an umbrella and said, "Come on, I'll pull you up."

I didn't care who helped me just as long as I escaped that dog at my heels, and I figured I might even be able to have a little fun with this doll. But when I grabbed that umbrella, I didn't go up toward the woman. Instead, I started moving straight down, toward the dog, who was waiting for me with open

101

jaws. And when I looked back up, the beautiful woman wasn't so beautiful anymore. She had turned into an ugly, cackling hag.

That dream scared me out of my mind. I woke up in a cold sweat and painted the entire downstairs of my mother's house in one day without stopping. The dream bothered me so much I told Mom about it, and she warned, ''Son, Satan is after you. Give your life to Jesus.''

But I wasn't ready for that. I might have been thrown off stride a little by a bad dream, but I was still Nick the Greek, the devil's son-in-law. If Satan was after me, I'd use him as much as he used me. That was the way I thought. My mind, my judgment were distorted. My life had accelerated to the point where I was just along for the ride. I'd made my main choices long ago. I'd used women any way I wanted for my own pleasure. I'd manipulated men to increase my power. Drink was changing me into a crazy man as I shot, knifed, and clubbed anybody I pleased. Violence and blood were the dessert of life for me. I had joked about selling my soul to the devil. But the joke had finally become reality. I had become more than just my father's son, as bad as that might be. I was Satan's son now. My career in crime had peaked at such a precarious height that I couldn't keep my balance any longer. I had no control over myself or my destiny.

That was when my life fell completely apart.

You remember that very first story I told you about how I bet on a pinball game with an out-of-town pimp in a Cleveland bar? And how I got shot in the head when the pimp slugged me with his Luger? Now, maybe you understand a little better how something like that could happen to me.

The pain, the physical pain, started to get really

bad with the gunshot in the head, and it kept getting worse — especially when those two hit men caught up with me during that car chase and then beat me up so bad. I can't tell you how much I was hurting, walking around with those half-open wounds. But maybe you also understand a little better now why I had to buy drugs to kill the unbearable pain — and why I naturally turned to armed robbery to get the money I needed.

I was half-crazy *before* I got shot and beat up, with all the boozing and fighting and stealing I was doing. The wounds just made it ten times worse. I was short on judgment before I got hurt. But when I had to walk around with the top of my head gushing blood and my face aching from the punches and kicks of those hit men, I found I had no judgment at all.

It was easy for somebody in my condition to get involved in one robbery too many. And that's exactly what happened when my partners and I held up that grocery store and then got caught right afterward by those cops who surrounded us in dozens of squad cars. At that point, my thinking was totally distorted from the physical pain and from my sick criminal mindset. I don't think I could have foreseen that this robbery would have been my undoing, even if a bunch of cops had been waiting inside that grocery store with their guns drawn. That's how blind I was to what was happening to me, and to the downward slide that was rushing me toward an inevitable, devastating crack-up of my whole life.

After I got arrested, I was thrown in the county jail and finally sentenced to a minimum of ten years in prison. You already know about all that. So maybe now you understand better some of the things that were going through my mind in that hospital ward, as I bent over on my knees and tried, for the first time in my adult life, to talk to God.

A kind of movie was playing in my mind as I knelt

on the prison floor that night, and it wouldn't quit. It was worse than any triple-X film, but I couldn't stop it, even when my wounds started aching unbearably and my stomach started to turn. Something, or Someone, was compelling me to watch. I had to sit right there and face every dirty thing I'd ever done, in all the terrible detail.

I hadn't taken time to reflect on the garbage world this way before. And I hadn't taken a really good look at all the evil I'd done. But now I didn't seem to have any choice. And in a way, I really *wanted* to get it all out on the table. All my past deeds were laid out there before me and then were being crammed right back down my throat, just as I'd often forced others to do things against their wills. Something I didn't quite understand was happening to me, and I sensed I'd have to wait till the end of the mental show I was viewing to get the complete message. So I settled back, gritted my teeth and kept watching the garbage spew forth out of my little black Greek heart.

7

The Final Fork

As I knelt there on that cold prison hospital floor, the jeers of the other inmates kept ringing in my ears:

"Hey, Greek, you going to become a Jesus freak?"

"Hey, Greek, you lost something down there?"

"Hey, Greek, you trying to get religion?"

I was aware of what they were saying. But for the first time in my life, I didn't care. I was used to going on instinct . . . used to cutting people on instinct . . . used to stealing on instinct. But now as I crouched over with my eyes closed, my instincts weren't working anymore. All that I cared about was watching that movie inside my brain. It seemed as if somebody had reached into my guts and flipped some kind of light switch. Now I could see things I'd never seen before; I could look at the people and situations around me in a completely different way. I realized all of a sudden I'd forgotten what it was like not to worry about looking over my shoulder to see who might be trying to put me down or get the better of me. For a reason I couldn't understand, every scene of my past life that I relived made me a little looser, a little less defensive. And when that mental movie finally slowed to a halt, when I returned from the past to the present, I did something I hadn't done since I was a little kid.

I cried.

Right there in that prison hospital, with those other tough inmates close enough to touch me, I broke down and cried.

I sobbed, "Forgive me, Lord!" and then I just let a whole flood of tears come out. Some of those tears had been bottled up inside me since I was a child on the tiny island of Chios in Greece. After I had come to America, I had learned to push the agony and melancholy of my life deep inside myself. When I had cried, I had cried within. But now it felt good to be able to cry real tears, tears that flowed so freely they wet that rough prison floor.

And as I cried, I begged once again, "Lord, forgive me!" Over and over I prayed that. Then I said, "I promise you, if you give me one more chance in life, a new start, as long as this heart is beating and this tongue can wiggle up and down, I will speak of you. If you just give me another chance. . . ."

Suddenly, it felt like a great, warm hand reached into my insides and held me powerfully but gently. And a voice seemed to penetrate down deep where all that garbage had been, a voice that said, "Yes, I *will* that thou would be whole! I *will* that thou would be whole, Nick!"

At that moment, something just lifted inside me. I didn't understand it, but I knew, somehow, that in spite of all I'd done, I was forgiven. I was clean. And I finally had a father—a *real* Father, who loved me and accepted me, just as I was, a lowly and undeserving prison inmate.

It felt so good to take the next breath, almost like I was smelling the fresh clean sea air of Chios for the first time in more than a decade. It felt so good to stay down there on the floor, crying and praying and crying some more. I wasn't the kind of guy who got down on my knees for anybody. You know that. But I was more comfortable in that position than I'd ever been sitting or standing or running anywhere else in my whole life. I asked God to forgive me for every single thing I could remember I had done wrong. That was a lot of things and it took a lot of time.

When I finally raised my head, it was dark in the hospital ward. Only the night lights were on, and everybody — each one of those inmates who had been laughing at me — was sound asleep. I crawled into bed a happy and relaxed young man that night. But I didn't go to sleep. My mind was still working overtime, still putting out images, only this time I wasn't watching or hearing garbage. This time I was looking at how many times God had saved me from myself in the last few years. I saw how a knife had just grazed me, or a fist quit pounding my head just soon enough, or a pistol misfired, or a bullet just missed the mark. The way I survived those close calls had nothing to do with me or luck or coincidence. It was God's mercy and my poor mother's patient prayers that had kept me alive for this moment I was experiencing now.

Every now and then, a hospital orderly would come through and tap me on the shoulder through the covers and ask, "Hey, Greek, want some medicine?"

"Hey, man, leave me alone," I said. I didn't want to be bothered, not now. These guys were breaking into this beautiful thing that was going on inside me. You know how your stomach growls sometimes and you can't stop it? Well, that's like this thing that was going on inside me, but this was a happy bubbling feeling that wouldn't quit, and I didn't want to stop it.

When the first rays of morning arrived, my mind started to slow down. Finally it stopped. I lay there quietly in my bed, just enjoying the feeling of being clean through and through for the first time in my adult life. And I prayed, "God, wouldn't it be great, really great, if I could see that Super Mexican, Ernie Lavato, the Christian who got me started on this thing, and let him know I prayed this prayer?"

The moment I said that in my heart, a guard came through the door, walked up to me and said, "83284, you got a pass."

I looked at that pass and it told me to go to the X-ray room, where Ernie was assigned. I was so happy I just wanted to fly down the four flights of steps, just run down them four at a time in nothing but the underwear I was wearing. But the rule says you have to take an elevator and be properly dressed, so I quickly combed my hair, washed my face, put on my little hospital dress and went outside and waited for the elevator.

When I got to Ernie's floor and the elevator opened, I heard a big old wooden radio playing loudly down there, and I didn't notice at first that some preacher was speaking. But then the preacher said in a loud and clear voice, "And God. . . ." and he hesitated. And goose pimples popped up all over my back. It dawned on me as I heard those words that I had combed my hair, washed my face, and walked to the elevator that morning—but I had felt no pain! I touched my face and the top of my head where I had been wounded, and I pressed harder and harder. But there was no pain! I was healed! God had healed me!

"Ernie, he's real and alive!" I shouted at the top of my lungs.

And all of a sudden Ernie came out from behind a stack of records. But I couldn't stand still and talk to him, I was so excited. I ran up and down the X-ray room screaming about how great God was and how Jesus Christ was now at the center of my life. "Praise God, Ernie! Praise Jesus for what he's done for me!"

Ernie kept running around behind me, trying to calm me down because he was afraid I was going to pass out on him. But when it finally dawned on him what had happened, he started shouting, "Praise God!" too. And we began dancing around the X-ray room, thanking God together.

Two guards who had been posted outside heard the commotion and rushed in to see what was happening. But the presence of God was so real and powerful in that room, they didn't need much of an explanation. The walls and machines seemed to want to jump up and down with us and give praise to God. Before I knew it, they were crying and praising God right along with us.

I didn't want to go back to my hospital ward. I just wanted to stay down there in that X-ray room with Ernie and praise God all day long. But things don't work that way in prison. I might have established a relationship with Jesus Christ. A dramatic change might have taken place in my life. But most of the prison authorities could care less. They wanted everything in order, everybody in his proper place. So that meant I had to go right back to my hospital bunk and continue my ordinary routine as a prison inmate — even though now I was a completely different man, with a different way of feeling inside.

It was a happy, excited feeling, but it was also a little scary. I could sense God near me now, and I knew he was going to have to get involved in the decisions I made in the future. But I had no idea he was going to get involved as soon as he did. Only a few minutes after I stretched out on my bunk, one of my doctors walked up to me and asked, "You ready to decide?"

"Decide what?" I said. I'd already made all the decisions I wanted to make that day.

"About the operation on your head," he said.

Nick the Greek

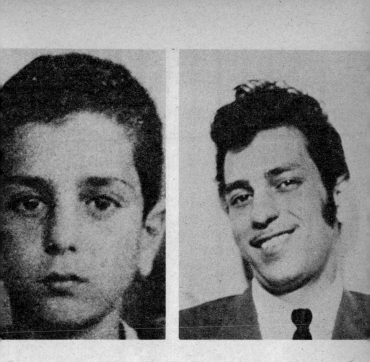

Ten-year old Nick not long after immigrating
to the U.S.

Nick as a teenager.

One month after his release, Nick gives a friendly
handshake to a lawman.

NAME: PIROVOLOS, Nicholas
Institution & No. OSR 83 284
County Sentenced: Lorain
Crime: Armed Robbery
Admitted: 1/20/72   Term: 10-25
Paroled:
Length of Parole: One Year
Max. Exp. Date: 11/2/96
Criminal Record: BCI# A 515 571
                 FBI# 888 141 E
                 CPD# 120 197

S.S.# 270-42-7713

Age: 2/16/47   Height: 5'6½"   Weight: 135
Marital Status: Married   Occupation:
Physical Condition: Good
Home Address: 9640 Pleasant Lake Blvd
              Parma, Ohio   13173 JACQUED
                            Strongsville - 237-673

Sponsor: Mrs. Dottie Pirovolos (wife)
Address: same   Phone No. 886-6073
                                                88-
                                                8299

Employer:
Address: Phone No.

Relatives & Address: NO PROBLEM
                     HE IS A CHRISTIAN

This field report records a parole officer's
evaluation of Nick's life-style and behavior: "No
problem. He is a Christian."

A young inmate in Knoxville prison is sentenced to die in the electric chair, but is set free by Jesus.

Top: He is no respector of persons. Whomever God sets free is free indeed!

Bottom: As a counselor with the Bill Glass Crusades, Nick shares the gospel over lunch in the Florida State Prison.

Top: "As I'm sharing Jesus, I let them feel the crease in my head from the bullet wound so that they know I'm not telling them a bunch of fairy tales. . . ."

Bottom: You cannot fool an inmate. When the truth is shared, they accept it. They accept Nick because he was once one of them.

Bill Glass speaks at a prison crusade.

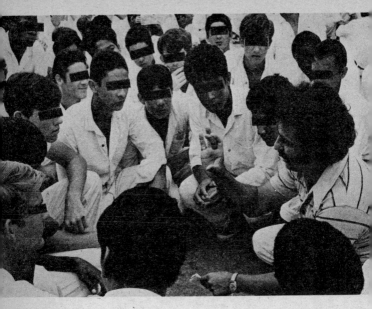

Inmates in Texas. Nick says, "It is amazing how God is using me. Their eyes are fixed on me. They see Christ. God uses my past to bring him glory."

A U.S. admiral (left), Charlie Waters of the Dallas
Cowboys (center), and Nick the Greek (right)
sharing together in a prison ministry.

Nick, Dottie, and four-year-old Nicole.

Top: A notorious criminal finds freedom in Christ. He is serving a life sentence and sharing the hope that he has in Jesus.

Bottom: Nick with Dr. Kenneth Taylor, paraphraser of *The Living Bible*. The Bible Nick is holding is the same *Living Bible* he was given when he was in prison.

Then I remembered. They had given me a couple of days to think about whether or not I wanted them to cut into my skull to see if they could find what it was that was causing the pressure and pain in my head.

"My decision is already made," I said, "Jesus Christ healed me. That's my decision."

"What?" he said.

I put my hands up to the spots that had been the most tender on my head and I pressed hard. "Don't you see?" I asked. "God healed me!"

The doctor didn't say anything for a couple of seconds. He looked like he couldn't believe what he was hearing. "That's incredible," he finally said.

"Yep, you're right. It's incredible. But it happened."

"But we'd still like to go inside your head and find out what's happening there," the doctor said. He obviously didn't believe my story completely.

"No, you ain't going to cut," I said, and that was that. They had to have my permission to operate, and I wasn't about to give it to them.

But they did take some X-rays after my healing, and those pictures showed that physically, everything was just the same inside my head. The difference was that I continued to feel no pain. According to the X-rays, I *should* have felt pain, but I didn't. I could taste food again, too.

I had regular check-ups after that, and every time the doctors would tell me, "We don't see how you're even living. By all rights, you should at least be in pain, hurting."

And they were right. Before my encounter with God, I had to take enough medicine to tranquilize an elephant. Even a slight coldness or dampness would cause such pain that my whole face would become numb. Half the time, I had to walk around with a handkerchief pressed against my eye to lessen some of the pain. But no more. I didn't hurt at all any more.

Finally, the doctors gave up and accepted me at my word. They decided I wasn't sick any more, and they arranged to have me transferred to a regular prison cell at the Ohio State Pen until they could send me back to Mansfield. The only cells available for me at the time were in the death row block, where they kept the guys they were going to barbecue in the electric chair. But I didn't really care where I was going, because now I knew I wouldn't be alone. God was going with me.

I felt even better about the move when Ernie, the Super-Mex, came up to me after he learned about my transfer. "Greek, just remember one thing," he said. "Don't forsake the Lord, and he will not forsake you. He will never leave you. There's a verse in the Bible, Proverbs 3:5, 6, I want you to keep in mind when you leave here. . . ." He then pulled out a little Bible he carried around with him and read, "Trust in the Lord with all thine heart; and lean not unto thine own understanding. In all the ways acknowledge him, and he shall direct thy paths."

Then he reached into a bag he was carrying and took out a little flat box and handed it to me. "This is yours," he said. It was a new Bible. I had never read the Bible in my life. I had never even owned one. It had never crossed my mind to get a Bible before because in the first place, I didn't read beyond a first or second grade level, and in the second place, I hadn't cared a thing about God. But now all that had changed. Now, I *did* care about God and his Son, and I wanted to know more about spiritual things. I might not be able to read any better, but one way or another I was going to learn. You could bet on that. If God could take away my pain, he could certainly teach me how to read a book.

So as Super-Mex and I stood facing one another

that day, just before I left for death row, we didn't have to speak. We understood each other perfectly. I didn't know what the next few years had in store for me, other than the fact that I'd have to deal with one of the toughest prison situations in the country — from the inside looking out. But I did know God was going to be with me because during that night I had spent on my knees, I had taken the final fork on the rocky road of my short life and found I still had a future of some sort. If I had taken the wrong route that evening, I'd have faced a dead end, and maybe even death itself. But now a path stretched out in front of me, and I was determined to follow it, no matter where it led. I was already feeling a breeze of freedom sweeping past me, and even though this sense of liberation was different from anything I'd ever known before, I didn't care. I wanted as much of it as I could get, even if I had to learn my first lessons in freedom in the most "un-free" spot in all the world — death row in the Ohio State Pen.

8
Freedom
Behind Bars

I had been looking for freedom all my life. I had tried sex, liquor, travel, violence, robbery, you name it. But the more I looked and the faster I lived, the less free I seemed to become.

That night on the floor of that prison hospital, I found freedom, but not in the place I'd expected. My search had always focused on bringing things and people under my power, but somehow, I'd never thought to check inside myself. And of course, that's exactly where God first directed my vision — deep into the dirty abyss I had created in my heart and mind with all the crimes I had committed.

When I allowed Jesus Christ to enter every dark corner of my inner being and scour away all the dirtiness and inadequacy with his forgiveness and take complete control of my life, that's when I found true freedom — a freedom *within*. As I lay on my bunk that first night on death row, after I'd been released from the prison hospital, I experienced real happiness for the first time in my life. If anybody had tried to tell me what a total commitment to God could do for me before I had actually experienced it, I'd have laughed at him. Or punched him out. But now that I was getting a strong taste of this inner freedom only God can provide, I found myself wanting more and more of it.

Those bars I sometimes stared at on the door of my cell didn't mean a thing now. I didn't even care that I was still in prison, because in a very real sense, I *wasn't* in prison. I was a free man down deep inside, a free man who could feel peace and happiness and contentment no matter what outside pressures were bearing down on his mind and body.

I suspected the prison authorities had put me on death row to give me a hard time, and maybe scare me back into my pain. They knew the things I had done and they knew I was anything but a model inmate, even though I'd been in prison for only a few months. So I'm sure it stuck in the craw of some of the guards that all of a sudden I seemed to be a happy guy who wasn't a bit concerned about having to do time.

But if they had put me on death row out of spite, they must have been very disappointed in the way I reacted. For me, the solitude was a real blessing, and the experience turned into sort of a spiritual retreat. For the first time in my life, I slept like a baby. Before my encounter with God, I slept like a wild animal — lightly, on edge, ready to spring into action when there was even the whiff of danger in the air. But now that I'd put my life and future in God's hands, I just relaxed. No words can adequately express the joy, peace, and forgiveness I felt in those first days on death row.

The only pain I remember feeling was a dull ache in my side — an ache caused by the fact I slept every night with that little Bible that Ernie Lavato had given me tucked securely under my body. I was afraid to lose contact with that book because it had become my lifeline to the increased sense of freedom that was enveloping me. It's not that I could read it very well. In fact, I couldn't read most of it at all. But that Bible became my ticket to learning how to read and write, and the more literate I became, the more deeply I could delve into that free world of the Spirit that I longed to know more about.

Here's the way I worked with that Bible: It was a "marked Bible," which told me what page to start on and then referred me to more truths and promises. I copied many verses down, word for word, in a spiral notebook I'd gotten from somewhere. Even when I didn't understand the meaning of many of the words, I'd write them down anyway.

And then I'd say to God, "This is my prayer, and I claim it for my own life."

Finally, I'd speak those words out loud over and over again, phonetically. I didn't pronounce most of the words correctly, but I said them anyhow. And I prayed, "God, I want you to show me what's in this book. I want to be able to understand."

And it was amazing, but as I moved from one passage to the next, I would literally start to see what he was saying. I would see those donkeys and animals moving around, and the women walking around in their veils and the men acting however the Bible said they were supposed to act. I could also hear my grandmother and my mother and my sister reading the Bible in Greek and telling those Old and New Testament stories, back there on the island of Chios. It all started coming back to me as I got deeper and deeper into studying God's Word. I know now the Spirit was tying all this together for me so I'd understand.

The Bible Ernie had given me was *The Living Bible,* an easy-to-read modern English version. Not only did this little Bible teach me about God, but it taught me English as well. An English word or phrase that I recognized would tip me off about what the general story line was, and then gradually I'd put the English words I didn't know together with the Bible stories I'd heard as a boy. Finally, it would all fall into place. So that's how I learned to read and write — and speak — English. Human beings had tried to teach me, but they had failed. God, though, never fails, not even with Nick the Greek.

I also learned spelling the same way. When I was trying to write something down in a letter and I found I needed a word I couldn't spell, I'd think, "Oh, I just read that in chapter five." So I'd look it up for the spelling. I gave up many meals on death row because I didn't want to lose a minute's time in this school of the Spirit I had entered. Some of the other inmates thought I was kind of a crackpot, so they took to jeering at me now and then and throwing bits of paper and cigarette butts into my cell when they walked past. But I hardly even noticed them. And sometimes the trash they tossed did me more good than harm. A lot of the stuff advertised free religious literature and Bibles, so I took a close look at everything they threw at me. But to my surprise, not all the inmates thought I was a crackpot. The positive response to my new faith was as great as the hostility. I only spent a month on death row, but I found that even in that short period of time, I became a kind of magnet for those who were starved for spiritual food. There I was, a baby Christian, almost totally illiterate, with a sparse knowledge of the Scriptures, and other inmates looking for spiritual guidance started coming up to me in the mess hall when I tore myself away from the Bible to get some food. That was hard for me to believe. And it was often frustrating and frightening.

Many times, one of them would ask me a simple question: "How do you know Jesus can forgive sins? Did he ever say he could?" And I wouldn't be able to put my finger right on a verse — mainly because I couldn't read well enough to find the right passage.

So I'd go back to my cell that night and cry, "God, help me!"

I wanted so much to give answers to those who asked me questions about Christ. I had always had the answers when guys would come up to me and try to hire me for some crime. But those requests to do violence to others had never meant so much to me as the questions I was now getting. And yet, I was much less qualified now to give any kind of spiritual advice than I had been to pull off a robbery.

Still, as poorly prepared as I was, God did respond and help me. I often went to sleep with a song echoing in my mind because I was beginning to learn the miraculous ways God could talk to me and guide me. In my case, he taught me a lot through my dreams. An inmate might have put a question to me, and then I'd drift off to sleep and I'd start dreaming that Jesus Christ was beside me. We'd be walking down a sidewalk, and the wall or fence next to us would be filled with Scriptures. And he would say, "Nick, this means this, and this means that." And I'd say, "Wow, I've got to remember this when I wake up!"

Then the next morning, during breakfast, I'd run over to the inmate who had asked me the question, and I'd tell him the very answer he had been looking for.

Soon after I had decided to follow God instead of myself, I got a visit from my mother. I had written her something about what had happened to me — I could write Greek, even though I only had a first-grader's knowledge of English. But I don't think she really believed me at first. In fact, I think she came to see me just to see whether I was trying another con job.

One of my sisters brought her to the prison, and when we got settled in the visitors room, I didn't give them much of a chance to say anything. I just ran off at the mouth, telling them about all that had happened to me in the hospital ward, and I jumped up and down in front of them, gesturing like a wild man.

"Is there anything we can do for you, Nick?" my sister asked, apparently a little concerned that I had gone completely off my rocker.

"Just a cross!" I said. "Get me a cross!"

That seemed to convince my mother a little bit. "Thank you, Lord!" she said. "It's a miracle."

"I'm healed, too, Mom!" I said, pointing to my head, where I had been shot and kicked.

"How long is it going to last?" she asked, shaking her head, not quite willing to believe the rotten son she had given up on a couple of months before had done a complete about-face. I know she had heard this kind of conversion could occur. She knew the story of Paul in the Acts of the Apostles better than I did. But in her own family? With a son like me? She wasn't going to jump to any final conclusions just yet—and I didn't blame her!

But it was a real thing with me. I knew that by the way I felt inside. I was a very new Christian. And the change in me had been abrupt—so abrupt that I knew the force for change had to come from outside me, from God. There was no way I could have changed that quickly and completely on my own.

But I don't mean to give you the impression I had become some kind of saint overnight. I had a long way to go—much longer than I realized while I was doing my time on death row. Since I had trouble reading the English Bible Ernie had given me, there was a lot I didn't understand about how a Christian was supposed to act and believe and relate to God. In fact, as far as I knew, Ernie and I were the only followers of Christ in the prison system.

When the authorities in the Ohio State Pen finally decided I really had been healed and could do my time like any regular inmate, they transferred me back to Mansfield. Apparently, the word was getting around about what had happened to me, because in the truck that transported me back to Mansfield, I was handcuffed to a Hell's Angel who somehow knew about my conversion.

"Hey, Greek, we hear you got religion!" he said. "What is this, man? You turning into a squaw, an old woman?"

Now, this guy was one of the ugliest looking guys I ever met. He had some kind of skin disease, and his body was covered with scars and lumps and tattoos. Also, he had poisoned his body for years with dope, and that gave his face and eyes a vacant, kind of crazy look.

A few months ago, I wouldn't have asked any questions. I would have distracted him some way and then coco-butted him right in the face. But now, somehow, I was different inside. I didn't react in my old way. "Man, in the past I'd tear you apart for saying that," I said. "You don't know me very well, or you wouldn't talk like that. But instead I'm going to tell you about what Jesus Christ has done in my life. . . ."

And then I told him exactly what had happened to me in the hospital ward, and all the while I was gesturing in his face with my Bible. I thought the Bible was magic, that it gave some sort of special power, like a wand or something, so I kept it right out there in plain sight.

Finally, the Hell's Angel noticed it and asked, "Let me read that."

"No, man," I said. "You're too dirty. This is a holy book, God's Word."

He cursed at me, but he didn't make any move to

take it away from me and I was glad for that because I would have fought him for it. Where I come from in Greece, you don't touch the Bible with your fingers. You kiss it sometimes and bless it. But you don't touch it like any other book. That's the way my mind worked in those first few weeks after I accepted Christ. I had nobody to tell me otherwise, so when I faced a tough decision about my new faith and couldn't find the answers in the Scriptures, I just fell back on my old Greek religious tradition.

They stuck me and this Hell's Angel in the same cell when we got to Mansfield — an old, dirty, out-of-the way place that must have been reserved for the worst inmates. But I didn't really care because the Spirit of God was still doing some exciting things inside me, showing me how to pray and how to read the Bible in English. My "celly," the Hell's Angel, kept bugging me, though. He said, "Hey, man, tell me more about this Jesus stuff." And he kept asking me to let him read my Bible. "You can trust me, Greek," he said.

Finally, I gave in and let him look at it. The next day, he was transferred to another cell and then he was released early from prison on what's called "shock probation" — and he took my Bible with him. He stole my Bible! I was ready to kill him. That Bible was the only book I had ever read from cover to cover in my life, and I loved it as much as I loved any human being.

I was really steaming for a few days after that, and it's lucky that guy didn't come back because I don't know what I might have done to him. I was lost without my Bible. I didn't have anything to do except think black thoughts about that cellmate. But then I got transferred to a new cell, Cell 5, 2 N.W., and I noticed one of the bunks looked a little out of kilter.

When I looked to see what was causing the crooked-ness, I saw something had been wedged under one of the steel arms that support the bunk. When I checked closer, I found a little black Gideon Bible, with the New Testament, Psalms, and Proverbs!

I picked up that little book, stared at it for a couple of moments, and then started crying. God would take care of me — I saw that clearly now. I didn't have to worry about some guy stealing my Bible, because God would always provide another. But Bibles were so hard to come by in that prison that I decided I'd watch it very closely just the same. I stuck it in my pocket and kept it with me everywhere I went. The food I got from those pocket Scriptures was the best food I ate at Mansfield, and I wanted to be sure I always had it handy when I felt the need for some spiritual refreshment.

And here's a little footnote to the spiritual lesson I learned from that stolen Bible incident: That Hell's Angel who had run off with my Bible ended up back at Mansfield on another charge a few months later. But it turned out he had been going through some inner turmoil himself. He eventually became a Christian. I did a Bible study with him — and after that we didn't have to worry about him stealing anybody else's Bible. As a matter of fact, in the years I did time there at Mansfield, I kept running into inmates who had been helped into a relationship with God by this same guy.

But I'm getting ahead of myself again. Even though I had found another Bible, I was still at the very beginning of my relationship with God. I knew nothing about how to live the Christian life or how to share my faith with others. There was this one guy I kept running into on my job in the prison. I was the cook for the guard officers, and this inmate would drift over beside me and start talking about religion. He was obviously interested, but everything he said was negative.

"You really believe this stuff, Greek?" he asked, pointing at my little black Bible.

"Yeah, I believe it," I said, and I tried to show him some verses that supported what I was trying to say.

But he just brushed me off and started cursing at me, using God's and Christ's names in vain.

"Don't you curse like that around me!" I said. "You keep talking like that, and you're going to have to deal with me."

Now, it's not that I used the best language myself. I had a foul mouth after I accepted Christ, and it took me a few months to learn to clean up my act. The first English words I had learned as a kid were curse words. They came out of my mouth as naturally as "How do you do," so I had to re-learn a lot of things about how to express myself in a clean and clear way.

But this guy's language bothered me because it was directed against God and the Bible and my faith. And I wasn't inclined to put up with that. But the guy wouldn't listen to me. He kept on cursing and making fun of my faith.

So I said, "You keep on cursing, and I'll show you what I'm going to do."

But he kept on spewing forth this nonsense, so I reverted to the old Nick. I held that little black Bible up as though I was reading it. And when that distracted him for a second, I hit him — pow! — right on the nose with the little book. His nose collapsed in a broken mess on his face, I had hit him so hard. And he started to bleed like a faucet. Both his eyes closed up, and they had to take him to the prison hospital to patch him up.

I felt bad I had done that to him. I may have been only a month or so old in Christ, but I knew I had done wrong. I couldn't figure out what had made me act like that, and the whole thing continued to bother me. But I really got upset a day or so later when I walked up to my cell and just as I was about to enter, I saw this same guy lying in my bunk with his head all bandaged up. He looked like a dead man, with all that tape over his eyes and nose. I stood outside my cell for a moment and stared at the guy through the bars. He's either going to kill me or I'm going to kill him, I thought. I got ready to fight him, even though I didn't want to fight. But when I walked into the cell, I didn't have a chance to say anything.

"Greek, if you believe in God that much — to do this to me — I want to know your God!" the guy said to me. "I want to know more about your Jesus."

It was obvious to me that the Holy Spirit had been working in his life and, somehow, in spite of my own tendency toward violence, had opened him up to the gospel. So I sat right down on my bunk with him, and we prayed for Jesus Christ to come into his life. He was my very first convert.

Now I know this may seem like a strange kind of evangelism. It's not your usual kind of altar call. But God works in strange ways, especially in a prison. And, like I said, I didn't know the usual way to share my faith with others. I didn't know anything about prison chaplains and Christian fellowships. I just knew a little bit about the Bible and a lot about how God was changing my life.

The next serious spiritual discussion I had with an inmate was almost as strange as the first. I was assigned this cellmate who wasn't too sympathetic to any kind of religion, especially Christianity. I never minded guys who didn't believe the same way I did, just as long as they would leave me alone. But this guy was on my back from the first moment he started bunking with me. I think he assumed that anybody who was into Christianity must also be a weakling. So he kept riding me, making fun of my Bible reading and my belief in God. I didn't want to get into another situation like the one where I'd broken the guy's nose, so I tried to ignore him. But it got harder and harder, especially when he started getting physical with me. That's the way some guys are. They want to push you as far as they can, to see just how much power they can wield over you by acting tough. I know. I was that way for twenty-five years.

Finally, I knew I had to draw the line or this guy would push me too far, so when he poked at me one time and tried to spin me around by my arm, I said, "Don't play around with me."

That was all I said. Short and to the point. I put him on notice, and I figured that if God wanted this thing to be settled peacefully, he would inform the guy some way that Nick the Greek was not a man to be taken lightly. But my celly kept coming on strong. When he started getting rough with me again, I said, "I told you, I don't play!"

And I grabbed him around the neck and stuck his head into the toilet in our cell and started flushing away. Every time the guy would come up for air, I'd push him back down into the water again. When I saw he had had enough, I stood up and said, "Now, you ready to listen to God's Word?"

I expected him to swear at me or try to punch me out, but he just looked at me kind of funny, like he didn't fully understand what had happened to him. And then he said yeah, he *would* like to know more about God's Word. I couldn't believe my ears. It was obvious that violence was a natural part of the life of most of my fellow inmates, just as it had been a natural part of my own life. So I decided maybe it was sometimes necessary to get tough and bang a few heads just to get their attention. That way, I'd be more likely to command their respect so they wouldn't become preoccupied with trying to push me around.

There are rules and regulations in every prison, and Mansfield was no exception. But down on the level where inmates live from day to day, the rules keep changing. There's a hierarchy of leaders and followers, or godfathers and soldiers. Inmates create their own social system — and that means creating their sets of laws and traditions which regulate the way they relate to each other. You have to be strong and bold to survive and flourish in prison. The weak automatically fall under the power of the strong. There's a power vacuum at the grassroots level in every prison, and the toughest inmates always step into that vacuum and take control.

This whole social setup presents problems for the Christian inmate. Jesus taught that we should turn the other cheek. But what if you're trying to function in a society that in effect has no law except the rule that all power goes to the strongest citizen? What if you're associating with those who are used to being violent and abusing people and pushing others around? Sometimes the only way you can control these tendencies is to become a law unto yourself and stand up to those who are relying on strong-arm methods.

It's a fine line to walk, between showing Christian love and invoking a sort of frontier justice when the tough guys begin to get out of hand. But I was learning. My problem was that there were definite limits to what I could learn so long as I remained isolated, away from any contact with other Christian inmates. But like I said, I didn't have any idea there *were* any other Christian inmates.

My situation at that point in my spiritual journey was like a bird that tries to fly with only two-thirds of its wing feathers. There were three things I needed to do to move ahead at top speed in developing my relationship with Christ: (1) study the Bible; (2) spend time alone in prayer with God; and (3) share faith experiences and pray with other believers. I was doing the first two pretty well, but the third wasn't a part of my life at all. So like that bird missing part of its wings, I might have been able to fly a little, but I couldn't reach my full spiritual potential without contact with other Christians.

God knew my deficiencies better than I did, I guess, because he finally forced me into a situation where I couldn't help but run into some other believers. I already told you I was working as a cook for the prison officers, and there were some real advantages to that job. I got to eat the best food in the place, and while that may seem to you like a luxury, it was really just a matter of being sure I stayed in good health. None of the prison meals were exactly gourmet dishes, and most of what the average inmate had was downright garbage. I can still remember finding one batch of salad full of little black balls I thought were raisins, but turned out to be cockroaches. And some of the other junk you found in the food isn't worth talking about. You'd get sick if I told you all the details. One of the ways one group of inmates could take revenge on another was to put things in the food. You can use your imagination here, and believe me, the worst things you can think of would only suggest how bad the food was sometimes.

So I felt lucky to be able to pick the meats and salads that were at least fresh and clean, even if they wouldn't win any prizes for fine cooking.

But even if the food was okay, the management was terrible. The supervisor in charge of me, was an ex-con who was also a homosexual. I once caught him on the floor with another guy in the storeroom where we kept our canned food, and he couldn't forgive me for that. Also, he got really irritated when he heard me talk about my faith to the other inmates in the kitchen. He kept telling me to shut up, but I wouldn't and that drove him crazy. There was nothing wrong with my cooking, so he couldn't get me for not doing my job. But he was always pushing me, egging me on, looking for me to slip up and make a mistake so he could run me up on some charge. And to make things even more difficult, he made sure I worked long hours and got little time off.

All this began to wear on my mind after a while. So when I did get an infrequent free day, I went off by myself — as much as you could in a prison — and tried to recoup my spiritual energy so I'd be prepared for the guy's next attack.

It was on one of those free days, when I was trying to find a little solitude, that I stumbled onto something that was to change my life in prison almost as much as I'd been changed by God on the floor of that prison hospital. I knew from my Bible reading that Jesus often withdrew for prayer and rest when the pressures of daily life started getting to him. The Gospel of Mark is full of examples of this kind of withdrawal; for example, when Jesus withdrew to pray well before daylight in Mark 1:35 and the disciples had to go out hunting for him to pull him back into the action of life. And then there was the time he dismissed the crowd of five thousand after feeding them on five loaves and two fishes, and then headed up a mountain to pray. I really like Christ's words just before performing this miracle of the loaves and fishes. He saw that his disciples were tired from their work, so he said, "Come away by yourselves to a lonely place and rest for a while."

I identified with that passage because it was exactly the advice I needed. Jesus was talking directly to me and my problems, right out of the Bible, just like I was reading a letter from him to me or an advice column in the daily newspaper. That's how important and immediate the Bible was to me. It was my own "Dear Jesus" question-and-answer column, the wisest rules to live by. But unlike the columnists in the newspaper, the advice from *my* Columnist always worked!

So I withdrew to quiet, remote sections of the prison yard whenever I got a chance, just to pray and read and think. And it was on one of those little walks that I stumbled into an out-of-the-way cubbyhole in the basement area of one of the buildings. I was suspicious of the place at first because I couldn't make out what the people down there were doing. My mother had been writing me regular letters since my spiritual about-face, and she warned *"matia deca,"* which is a Greek saying that means, "Have all ten of your eyes open!" In other words, keep on guard all the time so nobody will pull you off the right path in life.

And that's exactly what I did as I walked down into that room. I kept "all ten of my eyes open" and prepared to beat a fast retreat if I ran into any drug users or anybody else that could get me into trouble. Trouble I didn't need. I had enough of that with my supervisor in the kitchen.

But I didn't run into trouble. I ran into other Christians — a whole roomful of them! I almost went wild. I had never had contact with Christians and had never even gone to church since accepting Christ. And here I was in the middle of a whole bunch of other believers!

I spent a long time talking with them and sharing the faith. And one of them said, "Hey, Greek, the chaplain's having an all-night retreat tonight up in his office. Why don't you come?"

I wasn't so sure about that. I liked the idea of knowing other believers, but I had my own little schedule and I wasn't so crazy about having it disrupted. But finally they talked me into it, and it was one of the most important experiences I was to have in prison, not so much because of what we did but because of the people I met and the way I started getting involved in fellowship with other Christians. I came out of my shell that night as I started getting to know the chaplains and Christian inmates who were going to have a big impact on my prison existence. I met fifty believers there at the retreat in the chaplain's office. I never realized there were so many behind bars!

At one point that evening, I'll have to admit I began to wonder, "What am I doing here? These guys are not even Greek Orthodox!" But all of a sudden it didn't matter. They were Christians, and that did matter. They all loved the Lord the same way I did, and I decided then and there I had to get to know them better.

There were three guys who soon became close friends of mine — James Hawk, Cullen Thompson, and Randy Wood. And there was the Rev. Ben Sorg, the Protestant prison chaplain, an iron man of God who knew the Bible better than anybody I've ever met. He started teaching me some of his spiritual knowledge, and my growth as a Christian began to move along even faster.

We spent a lot of time praising God and singing hymns that night, and I didn't get a wink of sleep. So you can imagine I was a little tired when I reported for work the next morning. I was hoping for an easy day, but that wasn't to be. My supervisor showed up mean and drunk, and he obviously planned to take his bad mood out on me.

I happened to be playing some religious music on a radio I kept near me as I prepared the food that day, but he didn't like that at all. First of all, he wasn't too happy about the idea I might have something like a radio that would make my work a little more pleasant. Also, he was really upset that I had turned on a religious station, because he hated religion and made no secret of that fact.

I was putting batter on some steaks and whistling away with the music when he walked over and shouted, "Shut that thing off!"

I knew there was no arguing with him when he was drunk, but I at least wanted a chance to wipe the batter off my hands before I touched the dials on my radio. So I just said, "My hands are dirty," and I reached for a rag.

For some reason, that set him off. "Can you whip me?" he yelled.

He was trying to start a fight, but I knew if I spoke back to him he'd have put me in isolation, in the hole. So I didn't say a word. I just stared at him. Finally, he said, "You report upstairs! You want problems, I'll see you get some!"

But when I got upstairs, the captain on duty happened to be one who liked the way I conducted myself at work.

"Captain Sackman," I said, "you've got to get me away from that kitchen downstairs. Either that supervisor is going to hurt me or I'm going to hurt him."

"Where do you want to go, Greek?" he asked. "You got the best position in the whole institution!"

The long and short of it is that with the help of Captain Sackman and one of the chaplains, a Rev. Warren Shelton, I finally ended up as a clerk — actually a glorified janitor — in the chaplain's office. My job was to mop the floors and clean toilets, and as God is my witness, I scrubbed those floors and toilets to his glory. Here I was, Nick the Greek, the well-heeled con artist, the master of violence, the little man who could bully anybody into doing his dirty work for him — doing the dirtiest kind of work imaginable, and loving it!

I wouldn't have traded my job for any other in the whole wide world. I had forced guys to wash my socks and underwear when I was first put in the county jail after my arrest. Now I was flushing toilets for other people. But it was all pure joy because I was able to be around other Christians all the time, praising God with them and studying the Scriptures to my heart's content.

I ended up as a permanent clerk for all three chaplains — Rev. George Koerber, Rev. Ben Sorg, and Rev. Warren Shelton — even though I couldn't even spell the word "clerk." I didn't look like much those first few weeks as a chaplain's assistant. But God often seems to be interested in the worst and the least qualified people to carry out his purposes. Like I say, I didn't look as if I would amount to much when I first came into that chaplain's office and started cleaning toilets. But God shows his strength and power by using the weakest people, and that's what happened with me.

All the power plays and excitement I'd experienced as a criminal were nothing compared to the adventure I was about to embark on in the cause of Christ at the Mansfield prison.

9
Rough-
and-Tumble
Revivals

I started learning how to be tough and hard when I was just a little kid. That toughness, that close friendship with violence, didn't just disappear when I decided to commit my life to Christ. Instead, God took that rough, criminal core in my personality and used it to fashion a rather unusual two-fisted faith and ministry for me.

Now don't get me wrong. I'm not saying I stayed the same violent guy I was before my conversion. I certainly didn't run around coco-butting or threatening people at the drop of a hat. And my main method of evangelism wasn't to go around breaking noses with my Bible or flushing people's heads down toilets as I did with my first two converts. No, I changed and softened up a lot in those first weeks and months after receiving Christ, and I've continued to see the more compassionate side of my nature blossom in ways that would have embarrassed me in my days as an up-and-coming young mobster.

But still, no Christian can completely escape his old background, and I don't believe God wants us to deny who we are and where we've come from. He wants to use each of our peculiar personality traits to extend his Kingdom in new and exciting ways. And that's exactly what happened with me during those years I spent as an inmate at Mansfield.

I was a tough guy, and everybody knew it. And that reputation made my own commitment to Christ even more impressive. If it could happen to Nick the Greek, it could happen to anybody: that was often the way people thought. So despite my lack of formal education and my inability to speak English very well, I was actually operating from a position of strength as I prepared to embark on a personal ministry at Mansfield. I had credibility. People believed me because I had nothing to gain and everything to lose by claiming to be a Christian.

God knew my strengths and weaknesses much better than I did, and he took charge of my development in the Christian community just as he had done at my conversion and during those first few weeks when I got to know him through private prayer and Bible study on death row. I did such a good job as janitor in the chaplain's office that I was promoted, if that's the right word, to being a regular clerk for the Catholic chaplain and then a sort of office manager for the entire chaplain's office.

But I sensed I wouldn't end up in an administrative job. I had always loved mixing it up with people, one way or another. When I was into crime, my "mixing" might have involved breaking some heads or lifting some wallets. Now that I was into Christ, I still liked that one-to-one confrontation. But the purpose of it was to hammer the gospel rather than brass knuckles into the heads of other people.

The kick I got out of telling others about Christ eventually led me to get more and more involved in the coffeehouse ministry that had first introduced me to the Christian inmate network at Mansfield. I started spending more and more time in that basement hideaway, until finally I was completely in charge of it. Now I was really in my element. I had a base which I could use to capitalize on my greatest strengths, and I didn't waste a minute in taking advantage of the opportunity.

We provided coffee and music for any of the guys who wanted to drift down to the coffeehouse during their yard time. I did a lot of preaching and a lot of talking to these men individually. And many, many came into a relationship with Christ, often twenty-five or thirty in a single day.

After we got a decent group of inmates in there, I'd stand up and say, "Hey, you guys, you need Jesus Christ! Look at the games people play around here — the power game, the homosexual game. Is that the kind of game you want to play? You may think everybody and everything in this prison is garbage, but God doesn't make garbage. His people are his children. They become garbage only when they let go of God.

"Look at yourselves, now, each of you. Look at what we've all made of our lives. But what's happened to me can happen to you too!"

Then I'd tell them some story from the Bible — maybe Samson or Solomon — and relate those passages in a practical way to their lives in prison. And I'd conclude by telling them, "God can forgive you, no matter what you've done or how often you've done it. How many of you have Christian mothers and dads praying at home for you? How many of you are from a Christian home?"

Then some would raise their hands and I'd start interacting with them and answer spiritual questions they might have. You'd always find a number of guys who were ready then and there to make a decision to follow Christ. So at the end of the session, I'd say, "I want those of you who want to receive Christ to pray with me right now. Stand up if you will.''

Then I'd have each of them repeat his name and number. I'd pray with him, and we'd immediately assign him to one of the prison Bible study groups that were organized out of the chaplain's office. There were many tears shed at those coffeehouse meetings, and many lives were changed. Soon, the word got around about what I was doing and how some of the toughest cases in the prison were finding meaning in life through Christ. Before I knew it, I had hardly any time to myself during the day. As I was walking from one part of the prison to another, guys would stop me umpteen times to tell me their problems. Sometimes, it got to the point where I couldn't deal with it. I couldn't sift through what they were saying, because I had heard and helped too much. "Oh, Greek, my wife is leaving me, can you help? . . . Oh, Greek, my son is sick, will you pray with me?''

On and on it went, and it wasn't just the inmates, either. The guards would pull me aside and say, "My wife is shacking up with other men . . . will you pray with me?'' They'd even come to my cell, as though I was keeping office hours for counseling, and ask, "Greek, I have this problem and I wonder if the Bible has something to say about it. . . .''

Sometimes, I actually had to shut my eyes and ears and run down the catwalks to get away from the people. I helped them all I could. I talked long hours with them and cried with them. But after a certain point, I couldn't handle it any more. I was weak and already operating beyond my physical and emotional limits only because the Holy Spirit was giving me extra power. But even with this supernatural help, there were times when I had to say, "No more!'' and just withdraw to catch my breath.

What it all came down to was that I knew there

were limits to what one man could do. I knew I needed help, but nobody else among the inmates felt called to do the kind of evangelism I was doing. And it had to be an inmate. The chaplains could do a lot of good, but there were simply many prisoners who couldn't identify with anybody in an official position. They figured, "What does a paid prison worker know about my problems? He's never looked at the inmate situation from the inside out!"

That was why I was in a good position to do the kind of personal evangelism and counseling I was doing — but I needed help. Desperately, I needed help. And help finally did come, but from a very unlikely quarter. There was a friend of mine from the old days, a guy named Orville, who got thrown into Mansfield on some charge. I don't remember exactly what he had done that time, and it doesn't really matter, because he had a police record a mile long. He had been arrested fifty-seven times, for all kinds of assorted crimes. He was typical of the friends I'd had in my old life.

I didn't even know he had been put in prison until one day I heard a knock on my door in the chaplain's office. When I opened it, there was Orville.

"Hey, Greek, what is this I been hearing about you?" he asked. "You turning into a Jesus freak? Is this thing for real, or you using it for the parole board?"

"Orville, it's real," I said. But I knew he didn't believe me. He was always looking for ways to get out of prison, and he thought my mind worked in the same way.

But he was curious. He kept staying close to me, checking me out like a coyote circles a campfire when a good piece of meat is roasting on a spit. That dog is afraid to come too close for fear he might get in trouble. But he knows he's smelling something beautiful,

149

and he wants to figure out some way to get a piece of it. That's the way Orville was with me.

He was as dangerous in prison as he'd ever been on the outside. Orville was a big guy, and on his first day in prison, he beat up four guys with a stool because they had jumped on some little inmate. He was a lot like I had been. He wasn't afraid of anything, and he was ready for a fight if you even looked hard at him.

But he couldn't figure me out at first. He even went so far as to pay one of the inmates who had an inside track to the warden's office to get his cell switched next to mine. He'd look at me inside my cell while I played my religious tapes and read the Bible. And occasionally he would walk in unannounced and thumb through my magazines, just to make sure I wasn't hiding a piece of porno or a *Playboy*.

He kept on probing and testing me. After he'd been in prison for a few weeks, he tapped into many of the illegal channels of contraband, like booze and drugs. And then he'd send me some liquor. But I'd send it back. Then he'd hand me some cocaine. But I handed it right back.

He really began to scratch his head because he knew what I'd been on the outside, and he knew I'd never turned any of those things down before. What had happened to me? Then Orville started coming to the coffeehouse and sitting in the back as I preached and talked to the other inmates. I knew he was ripe to make a commitment to Christ, but he always backed down when I brought up the subject.

It didn't help much either that he was rooming with a celly who professed to be a Christian, but who didn't live like one. This guy was always puffing on a marijuana cigarette and dealing in other contraband, even though he went to church on Sundays. Orville didn't have much use for him, and I can understand why. This guy represented what he had always thought religion was about—phoniness and hypocrisy. He was the worst kind of "Sunday Christian."

But there were enough real Christians around that prison to keep him wondering, so he was more or less ready to make a commitment. But then tragedy struck. I was on duty in the chaplain's office when I got a phone call, a death notice that his mother had died. She was the only person that had ever loved him. Orville had been a thief since the age of five, when his father would make him steal things so he could sell them to get money to spend on drink. But his mother always stood by him, and now she was gone.

I knew this was going to crush Orville, and I found myself wondering how God would allow something like this to happen, after I'd put in so much time moving him toward a commitment to Christ. As I expected, he didn't want to accept it. He wouldn't listen at first. Then his eyes glazed over and I could tell something important was happening inside him.

He was allowed to leave prison to attend her funeral if his family paid for a guard from the prison to go with him, and he didn't waste any time arranging that. But I could tell something was really wrong. Finally, he said just before he left, "Greek, this is the last time you'll be seeing me. I'm leaving, running."

It seemed he had a friend who was going to meet him outside with a gun, some money, and a car. They were going to jump the guard and keep on going.

"We'll be praying you won't do that," I said. "I know what it's like to be running from the man, with your head always turned around."

Anyway, he left and all that evening I prayed for him. I prayed, but I didn't hold out much hope. After all, what would I have done if I had been in his shoes? The time he was supposed to return passed, and I gave up on him. But I kept praying, just in case. Apparently, God had more faith in him than I did, because Orville finally showed up, late at night.

I knew he was back when I heard him in his cell beating up on his roommate, that Sunday Christian I told you about. There Orville was, on top of his celly, yelling, "Where does it say in the Bible that if I was to die this very moment, I'd go to hell? Where does it say that?"

Well, I shouted at them to break it up, and I told Orville where that passage was in the Bible. Then I went back to sleep and didn't think any more about it. Orville was back. That was all that counted.

The next morning, when we woke up for trash call to put our garbage out, the first thing I noticed about Orville was his face was glowing. "Now, I can understand what you mean," he said. "Last night I prayed for the Lord Jesus to come into my life."

That marked a big turning point in my own ministry as an inmate in that prison. Orville joined me in the coffeehouse. He became to me what Timothy was to Paul. I taught him everything I knew about the Bible and spiritual principles and the best ways to pass the gospel on to the inmates. And he became my right-hand man. Orville kept records on our work in the prison, and he found that during the years we operated that coffeehouse in Mansfield, we saw thousands receive Jesus Christ as their Savior. That may sound unbelievable with just two uneducated inmates working together, but it happened. All you had to do was come down to that coffeehouse on several consecutive days and see dozens of prisoners standing up and praying to receive Jesus each day. Some of them were behind bars for several years, like me. But others were short-timers, who only came in for a few months. We tried to get to all of them at least once with the gospel because we knew the power of the New Testament message would probably turn them around if they could hear it only one time.

But I'm not saying it was easy. We had our tense moments. Sometimes I faced as much danger as a Christian at Mansfield as I ever did as a thief and mugger on the outside.

For example, there was the day the word got around that eight straight razors were missing from the prison barber shop. Orville and I were both preaching in the coffeehouse that day, but we weren't really too concerned about the news — at least, not until I saw this one Black Muslim push a kid up against a wall near the door to the coffeehouse and stick one of those missing razors against his throat.

I was talking to the group when I saw that blade come out, but I didn't even finish the sentence I had started. I bolted to the back of the room, grabbed the Muslim with the blade, and threw him up against the wall. The only problem was now his blade was pushing against *my* stomach.

We had been very careful to keep the coffeehouse clean and peaceful because some of the guards would have liked nothing better than to close it down. They pulled regular surprise searches on us, but they never found any contraband. And Orville and I made sure there weren't any fights in the place.

We also knew a knifing would do us in quicker than anything. That's the reason I reacted as fast as I did, and now here I was with an unfriendly razor poking into my gut. Still, I wasn't about to let this Muslim scare me.

"You fool!" I said. "Because of you they may close this place down! This is the only place where there's a little heaven in hell, and you're trying to mess it up!"

By this time, seven of the Muslim's friends had

appeared behind him, and each was carrying one of the missing barbershop blades. But I wasn't without support either—Orville and Smitty, another Christian, were right beside me, and they kept saying to the Muslims, "I rebuke you in the name of Jesus!"

But that blade was still pressing against me, and I thought maybe my time had come. So I prayed a prayer, "Oh, Lord, into thy hands I commit my spirit! Lord Jesus, take my soul! Forgive me of all my sins now!"

Then a passage of Scripture popped into my mind, from 1 John 4:4, and I shouted at the Muslims, almost without thinking, "Greater is he that is in me than he that is in you! Give me that blade!"

The Muslim drew back, like he'd been slapped across the face. He didn't hand over the razor, but he did take it away from my stomach. Almost as fast as things had heated up, they now cooled down. The Muslim's friends drifted away, but he came inside and sat sullenly at the back of the room. We gave him a cup of coffee and I finished my preaching, but I sure didn't forget he was there. As I gave my closing prayer, I said, "I pray, God, that the man back there"—and I pointed to the Muslim—"won't be able to sleep or have any rest; I pray his life will be full of turmoil until he comes to know you as his Lord and Savior!"

When I ran into the guy the next day, his face was all puffed up from no sleep. And he said to me, "Greek, I can't go on like this. Would you lead me to Jesus Christ?"

And that's exactly what I did, right on the spot.

I found right at the beginning you had to use muscle, physical and mental muscle, on a lot of the inmates, just to get their attention. Sometimes I'd stand in front of those guys in the coffeehouse and say, "How many of you have the gall to stand up right now and say, 'Jesus, I receive you into my life?' Or is your spine made of Jello? You talk about being a man. But how many of you come in here and just play games, say how tough you was on the outside, how many women you had, how mean you was? But at night, you punch the walls because the mailman didn't bring you a letter from your loved one? You act so mean and tough, but you ain't tough at all!''

Rough words, I know. But some people, especially those in prison, don't understand reason. They only respond to force and power. And there's plenty of that in the gospel message, if we just learn to control and apply it.

I always kept my explanations of the plan of salvation fairly simple and relied on verses like Campus Crusade has in its ''Four Spiritual Laws,'' or the so-called ''Roman Road'' to explain how to receive Jesus. I'm talking about verses like Romans 3:23, Romans 6:23, and John 1:12.

But I found I also had to use a variety of tough, aggressive techniques that you have to know just to survive in prison. I would ask them, ''How many of you would be man enough to say you'll study the Bible for one week? If you scrape away the lousy mess that's covering your minds and bodies and take a good look at what's underneath, you'll see how much you need Jesus Christ. If you'll just put your name on this piece of paper, I'll put you in a Bible study, and you'll learn more than you ever imagined you could about God. And if you find after a month God is not as real as I say he is, then you can have a free fall on me. You get free punches against this body. But you got to be honest enough to say, for real, you're going to give your life to the Lord and not play games with him.''

A lot of guys responded to that direct, don't-play-games-with-me approach. And I never played the shrinking violet, no matter how big or rough a guy was supposed to be. Once when I was coming out of the mess hall, I heard this huge inmate making fun of God and us Christians.

I said, "You sound like the clown of the whole institution. You should go into show business."

There was always a chance a guy like this might try to punch me out right on the spot. But it never happened. In fact, he was interested enough to sit down and talk some more with me.

"You ought to stop making fun of God," I said.

"You're a bunch of religious freaks," he said.

Not exactly civilized conversation. But that was a typical opening for a serious discussion in prison.

"Why don't you serve God instead of yourself?" I asked and put my hand on his shoulder.

"You get your hand off me!" he said. "You're crowding me!"

But I saw even if his words were strong, his eyes were weak.

"Your God never answers prayers," he said.

"Why do you say that?"

"Because I asked God not to kill my father, but he died anyway."

"What is death anyway, but a door that opens to eternity?" I said. "You just have to decide where in eternity you're going, to heaven or hell. Besides, God didn't kill your father. It's appointed to all men to die."

We kept on talking about God, and as I got more into the points I was making, I started poking him in the stomach until he had to stand up and move back so he finally had his back against a wall.

"Don't you crowd me," he kept saying.

But I said, "You're a chicken, a coward. I'm not bumming cigarettes from you. I'm not trying to con you out of anything. I'm just a beggar coming to tell you, another beggar, where you can find some grace and peace in your life.''

I don't know what this guy finally decided about God. I finally lost track of him. But I do know he was thinking seriously, and that's one of the main things I was trying to get those inmates to do.

Sometimes, Christians would work in pairs. We'd use a variation on the old ''Mutt and Jeff'' technique that cops use when they're questioning a suspect. One of us would be nice and kind, and the other would be tough and apparently insensitive. If my Christian friends seemed to be getting nowhere in a gentle conversation with an inmate, I'd walk up and say, ''Don't waste your time with this guy! He's just playing games. He's playing with your head, your time.''

That would sometimes shock the non-Christian into realizing this talk about God was serious business. On many occasions, I'd come back an hour later and find the unbelieving inmate in tears, ready to receive Christ.

Some people, in hearing about this rough kind of evangelism, have objected, ''You ought to be more loving and gentle, like Jesus.''

But like I said once before, remember that a prison, on one level, is a lawless society. You have to set up your own government and your own system of justice. You can't operate the same way you do in many places on the outside.

One of the best examples of this was something that happened to a Christian friend of mine named ''Lefty'' in one of the bathrooms at Mansfield. He was a pretty tough guy, but a lot of people thought he must be soft because he was a Christian. So when he went in to take a shower one time, four guys cornered him and tried to commit homosexual rape against him. But he was called ''Lefty'' for good reason. As they moved toward him, he raised that left hand of his and said, "I'm going to sanctify you. I'm going to keep you from sinning!"

And he sent all four of them to the hospital. But that wasn't the end of it. He also went to visit them in the hospital and prayed for them. A seed of the gospel was planted, even if the way he had gone about it was kind of unusual.

Even though we leaned hard on some inmates and used our muscle when necessary to keep the peace, we saw as much success in changing the lives of prisoners as you could ever hope to see in any retraining or rehabilitation program. And the prison authorities recognized the good we were doing and gave us some breathing room because of our sincere motives and positive results in introducing many of the inmates to Christ.

But not all the officials were so happy with us. Some guards thought that I, in particular, had a little too much authority and freedom for an inmate, and they were always watching for me to slip up so they could bring me up on charges. Finally, this one guard who disliked me thought he had caught me red-handed. Because I spent a lot of time in the coffeehouse, Rev. Sorg decided he'd just give me the keys to the room so he and the other chaplains wouldn't have to run back and forth to lock and unlock the door. Generally speaking, inmates didn't have access to prison keys. But some of the ways that rule and many others might be applied in practice were unclear. It was up to the official who at any point in time was in charge of the special inmate or situation.

This one guard, though, didn't go one little bit for the idea of my carrying a key. So he figured if he chose his time carefully, he could get me on that count. He waited until Rev. Sorg was away on vacation, and then he struck. He caught me coming out of the coffeehouse after I had locked the door, and he took the key away from me.

"I'm gonna put you in the hole for this," he said.

So he started leading me from the yard down to the hole, and he began to swear at me and tell me about how he was going to see I got an extra year in jail for the offense.

But I just said, after he'd cursed me again, "Go wash your mouth out in Matthew, Mark, Luke, and John."

And that just made him angrier. Other inmates saw what was happening as we walked toward the hole, and word got around what this guard was doing to me. By the time we reached the entrance to the hole where inmates were put in isolation, several hundred prisoners were waiting there for us. As I looked around, I saw many of my Christian friends and also a lot of other guys whom I had talked to about the Lord and who liked to come to the coffeehouse.

"You take us too!" they yelled at the guard.

"Hey, Greek, we going to have fellowship in the hole!" they said. "We going to have a good time!"

With all these other inmates so excited, the guard got worried he might have a riot on his hands if he locked me up, so he took me back to my cell and said he was going to have a hearing for me on the charge of carrying that key around and being a threat to security. Sure enough, he was able to set up a hearing, and Rev. Sorg still hadn't returned to be able to speak up for me. I'm sure he knew Rev. Sorg was away, and he wanted to move quickly and get me punished before he got back.

But things didn't quite work out that way. I told the hearing officer exactly how I'd got the key from the chaplains, and he said, "I know you have the key, but I just wanted to know what you would say. If Chaplain

Sorg trusts you, you *are* trustworthy as far as I'm concerned.''

And right there in front of my eyes he ripped up the charges and told me I was free to go — and he put the key back in my hand.

The guard who had it in for me was waiting outside the hearing room, and he asked, with a kind of sneer, "How much time did you get, Greek?"

"Praise the Lord, brother!" I said. "The Lord is with me. I'm free to do God's work in the coffeehouse!" And then I held up the key in front of his eyes. After that, I never had any more trouble from him or any of the other guards about the coffeehouse.

Many of us prisoners who were Christians in Mansfield at that time had an incredibly real sense of God's power and presence in our lives. I think one of the reasons for this was that we lived almost like monks. We had plenty of pressures exerted on us by the non-believing inmates and guards. But our Christian community was so close-knit and many of us developed such spiritual discipline in our personal lives that we almost couldn't help but grow more mature in Christ. In some ways I think it's easier to show fast progress as a Christian in prison than on the outside because there are fewer distractions and temptations behind bars.

To give you some idea of what a typical day in prison was like for me, here's what my usual daily schedule looked like:

7:00 A.M. — wake up, praying and thanking God for the day, even before my feet hit the ground. Prayers continue for a half hour.

7:30–8:30 A.M. — answer trash pick-up call, shave and clean up, eat breakfast while asking the Lord to bless the food and maybe even turn what I was being served into food.

160

8:30–9:00 A.M. — pray with chaplains; devotions.

9:00–noon — to coffeehouse, make coffee, get music set up on record player, assign other Christian workers their daily tasks, preach and conduct Bible study with inmates who wander into coffeehouse.

noon–1 P.M. — skip lunch to attend Bible study conducted by Rev. Sorg in chaplain's office.

1:00–1:30 P.M. — pray with chaplains.

1:30–3:30 P.M. — preach and conduct Bible studies in coffeehouse.

3:30–4:00 P.M. — eat.

4:00–5:00 P.M. — locked in cell; read mail.

5:00–7:00 P.M. — nap.

7:00 P.M.–3:00 A.M. — write letters, read Bible, pray.

During this period I completed dozens of Bible studies offered through the mail, and I also memorized a lot of Scripture.

I said I lived like a monk, and now I guess you can see what I mean. Some days, with all the preaching and teaching of the Bible, in addition to my own personal studies, I'd be in contact with the Scriptures one way or another for twelve to as much as sixteen hours. Even when I wrote letters, I'd have the Bible right by my side to copy words I didn't know how to spell or short phrases and passages I wanted to quote to make a point. The old habit I'd cultivated on death row of learning to read and write from the Bible stuck with me during the entire time I was in prison.

But despite the fact that I was growing closer and closer to God and learning more and more about his Word, something was missing. Another person might not have felt any lack in his life at all. But I did, and I believe the feeling of incompleteness I had was placed there by God himself.

I had been a Christian in prison for about a year when this feeling started to gnaw inside me, and at the same time I was getting something of a reputation for the ministry I'd helped develop among the inmates. Four inmates had joined to form a group called "Cons for Christ." These men—Cullen Thompson, James Hawk, Randy Wood, and myself—were solid Christian leaders among the inmates, and we had all decided that we could have a bigger impact both inside and outside the prison if we set up a formal organization for our ministry. The idea of "Cons for Christ" immediately caught on in the outside press, and several newspapers ran big feature stories on us. That caused a lot of Christians on the outside to get more interested in the work that was going on in prison, and we found ourselves getting groups of people coming in to participate in services and fellowship with us.

I met many nice people at these gatherings, but I never had any close ties to people on the outside except my mother. But she couldn't get around so well, since she was getting older and couldn't speak English, and so we had to rely mainly on letters.

One inmate said, "Why you so happy, Greek? You never get any visits, and still you're happy."

He was right. I was happy because I had good Christian friends inside the prison, and also I was so close to Christ I sometimes thought he was the only friend I really needed.

But still, I began to develop that sense of being incomplete, and I thought, "Wouldn't it be great, God, if you would give me someone that loves you just as much as I do? Someone I could share my faith with, someone who would visit me on Saturdays, just like other people get visits?"

I didn't have any set ideas about how God might answer that prayer. I wasn't even so sure he would answer it. I was just asking him in the same way a child might ask a daddy he loves very much. So I made that request and then went about my business. And one of the first items of business was a visit by a big group of Christians from Parma, Ohio, on the outskirts of Cleveland.

Now, you have to understand something about me and Parma. I didn't like people from there when I was a kid because we were from the other side of town. I sometimes went to Parma, but it wasn't for a friendly visit. If I took a bus in Parma, I'd jump out of a back window so I wouldn't have to pay the driver. And my gang and I would run around the suburb and steal bicycles and then ride them back to the east side of Cleveland, where we lived.

I figured the people from Parma were sort of snooty. They were the kind of folks I suspected disinfected their garbage before they threw it out. So even though I was now a changed person, I still wasn't so excited about meeting a bunch of people from Parma. Since I was one of the leaders of Cons for Christ, I was expected to attend the meeting and be a good host. But still, I was the last person to show up in the prison chapel for the program.

After I took my seat, though, I had to admit that these Christians from Parma had something going for them. The first thing on the program was a song by an older woman, and she really did sing like an angel. I always let people know what I thought, so when that music began to move me, I shouted, ''Amen! Amen!'' They were making me happy, these Parma people. People started turning around to see who was saying all these ''amens,'' but I didn't care what they thought. I was just praising God and the gift he had given that singer, and I wasn't about to hold back just because some cautious Christians were checking me out.

Then a tall young woman stood up to give her testimony, and she said, "My name is Dottie Elliott. I'm a school teacher from Parma, a kindergarten teacher. . . ."

And right away, my stomach started doing flip-flops. When I heard her say she was a teacher, those flip-flops should have stopped. Any mention of a teacher always made me think of the teacher who hit me over the head with a dictionary. I had always thought the best school teachers were dead ones. But that obviously wasn't the case with this young woman.

As those flip-flops kept on in my stomach, I said under my breath, "What's happening to me?" Then I raised my hand and said, "I plead the blood of Jesus!" I was afraid something evil was happening inside me, and I wanted God to do something about it. But still, the flip-flops continued.

Meanwhile, this Dottie Elliott was getting a little disturbed about the noise I was making in the back. "Who is that guy with all the 'amens' in the back?" she asked.

"That's the Greek!" one of the inmates told her.

She remembered then that she was supposed to give some information for Cons for Christ to a Greek, but she wasn't so sure she wanted to get close enough to me to hand it over. She did, though. She walked right over to me after the meeting and gave me a list of names of people on the outside that inmates could write to. And the closer she got, the more upset my stomach became.

At first, I didn't know how to interpret all this turmoil inside me. But when I returned to my cell that night after the meeting, suddenly everything became clear. One way or another, Dottie Elliott was going to be my wife. That conviction grew in me when she and several other Christian girls visited me one Saturday because they had heard from my friend Cullen

Thompson that I never got any visitors.

Unfortunately, things weren't quite that clear in Dottie's mind, as I learned from some letter writing we did over the next few months. I might have been getting what I thought were straightforward divine messages about marriage, but the messages she was getting were sometimes different.

10

Love Letters from Prison

Hi Dottie,

I greet you in the most Precious name of our Lord and Savior Jesus Christ. May His Grace and Blessings be upon you and your loved ones for now and forever and ever.

I pray that you can read my writing and my spelling. Let me know how you make out with it. I received your letter and I received a big blessing from it. Yes, Dottie, Satan never once leaves us alone. I know that from experience. I am happy to know you liked my testimony. I meant to say no matter who we are or what we are, we are helpless without Jesus Christ. . . .

Say, I miss you people. When are you coming down again? I always get my soul lifted whenever you come down to share with us. You see, I really don't get many visits so it's always a good feeling when I see you people come down. I would like to get to know you and about you if you like, and if you want you can ask me any questions you like, either about me or about this place. I'd like to become a close friend with you. . . .

Please also remember us in your prayers. Prayers change things, praise God! Take care and may God's Holy Spirit guide you in all that you do.

Agapi kai erene!
Love and peace!
Nick

Hello Greek!

Me again. Just a note to say I'm praying for the brothers there to be sensitive and do a follow up on the crusade [the Bill Glass Evangelistic Association Prison Crusade].

Greek, I really feel close to you and the more I write and share, and the more we share ourselves, the closer I feel. Yet I'm concerned as to what to say. I think we are to feel super special to brothers and sisters — some more than others cause even Jesus had John as the beloved. But my concern is mostly over letting things build cause I desire to have someone who cares and that I know likes me in spite of myself. . . . I *do* think of you as a *super fine brother* and friend, but I don't know what you feel and if things are growing in a different way for you. Keep me posted — O.K.?

Love ya' lots,
Dottie

Hi Dottie, and Praise God! And Smile!

I just came back to my cell after seeing you, and I am so blessed! I want to write to you a few lines and share with you what's in my heart. First of all, thank you for coming down. God answered my prayer because I prayed that you would come down by yourself.

168

You see why. I always praise the Holy Name of our Lord!

He guides me and tells me what to do. You see, Dottie, I talk to Him about us. I said, Lord, I am in love with Dottie very much. I feel very close to her. I said, Lord, please grant it for us to get together, and Lord, let us both feel your loving arms around us both. I know I may not be so good with words, but I have feelings and I believe that if we keep our eyes on Him first, we shall be happy.

Dottie, how can I say it? You make me feel good and you make me feel at ease. I feel deep down inside that you and I can be happy going together. You and I are much alike. I don't write to any sister the way I write and talk to you. I pray that God our Heavenly Father grant for us to make it together. I need you and want to be by you. Not only do you make me happy, but also the Holy Spirit through you witnesses to me and blesses me and gives me courage. God made woman and man for them to get together and be for one another and care and love and share with each other. Share pain, share love, and share joy.

For every woman there is a man, and for every man there is a woman. I feel deep down that you are the one. I have to tell you what's in my heart. I like for you to know how I feel. . . . All I can say is I love you and I do need you very much. Yes, Christ comes first in my life and always I want to do His will. But now I feel led to write this letter. Dottie, you have been in my thoughts, in my prayers and in my dreams always. Please pray that Jesus gives you a sign for us both. Don't think that I am trying to put you in a bind or push you. I just share with you what I feel about you. I know you don't know very much about me. But Isaac didn't know nothing about his wife, either. I also believe that God has His own plan, just like Moses' life and in many others in the Holy Bible.

I am at this moment lying on my bed listening to the radio and writing this letter to you. I feel very strange inside of me, and I know that from thinking of you, the thought of you brightens my whole day. . . .

Love ya,
Nick

P.S. In case you don't know, this is a love letter.

Dear Nick —

My only concern right now is that I'm the only sister [in Christ] you've really met and shared with, and maybe you mistake a normal sister relationship for more since it is more than you've ever known before. But I run around and goof off and share with many brothers and sisters, and I can feel warm with them all sometimes. So when I'm excited and we are sharing Scripture, Jesus and fun things, I just pray they aren't given or taken wrong. I feel no worry whatsoever, but I might if I didn't write all this. . . . Anyway, again I feel good about you caring — where it goes is in His hands, and I pray I never be a stumbling block in any way, cause I *sure* would be sad if I did hurt you.

Love ya,
Dottie

Dear Dottie —

I couldn't find any more truthful person than you. You are very humble. No, Dottie, what I feel for you is stronger than a brother-sister relationship. I am very much in love with you. Christ knows how much. . . .

You are in my thoughts constantly. I have never felt like this before. I know it may seem real sudden to you how things are working out, but I believe that God has His plans for us. If I was a phony, I would have stayed in my place or approached you a different way. But I only say what I really feel—the truth. I would like to hear from you to tell me what you think of what I just shared with you. Please tell me what's in your heart, and if what you write back would hurt me, it's best to get hurt now, than later. If you decide that you would be happy going around with me, that would make me real happy. I like for both of us to be happy and blessed.

I pray I didn't come on too strong and scare you off. I just had to share this feeling with you. . . . I am sitting here writing this letter by candlelight, so if this letter seems real sloppy and mixed up, one reason is I can't see straight. As I sit here, many, many beautiful thoughts go through my head and if I was to write them all, there wouldn't be an end to this letter. So I better put this hot pen of mine down and call it quits (smile).

Love ya,
Nick

Hello Brother!

Right now, I respect you *very* much, and I *love* your honesty with God and others. However, maybe I can't expect the other [feelings] till I see you in a normal setting. Nick, remember all this is very new to me, and like I said, a miracle could happen, but I think this type of relationship will just grow by sharing and day-by-day living.

Maybe until I've shared goofin' off with you, I can't handle the ideas. Remember, I can't even imagine someone putting their arm around me, or holding my hand and saying, "I love you."

So could the prayer be that Jesus will keep your feelings down and let mine grow if it is to be? As far as you being hurt, just know, if it isn't to be, man and woman sharing, it isn't because of you or me but because Jesus knows there is something much finer. If you feel good around me and I'm the wrong one, can you imagine what the right person will be like?!

If an [immediate] answer is so important, I'm afraid I may be a little too important to you. I care very much about you and it's important to me that you care about me. But for now, all I can do is pray to know if I should pray for a sign.

Love you with a love that's in His hands,
Dottie

Dear Teach —

I know that you are not used to having someone telling you that they are in love with you, and I don't go around telling every girl that I am in love with them. Now, please don't get the wrong impression of what I am writing to you. I really respect what you say because I *know for sure that you are being led by our Lord!* I am so blessed to see you have a real cool head and let Christ lead you in all that you say and do. I spoke too fast by suggesting to you to look or ask for a sign. Dottie, there is no doubt in my heart or mind you are all right!

In Isaiah, there is a verse that says, "Wait upon the Lord!" I really apply that or go by it. I wait and wherever He leads, I shall go. All I can say now is wait upon the Lord. But remember my feelings for you. I do feel strongly in love with you. I don't know how this will go. But I pray that He will take us a long, long way together.

No, Dottie, you are not a stumbling block for me. You are more than I can explain. I have really received many blessings just by sharing with you more than anyone else. You are a real cool person and one that hears God, and *I know it's a miracle* that you and I have met.

Oh, yeah, please let me know when you are coming down again so I could be ready and shave and put clean socks on (smile, Teach!). Well, I think I ran this hot pen of mine long enough. . . .

Agape,
Nick

Hi Nick!

Well, I'm home and the trip was really fast 'cause I was deep in thought — one thought — us! Nick, above anything else I don't want to hurt you, and in you I see more honesty than in anyone else I know. Please believe me that I believe you — everything you say. And God help me if I've let my wandering dreams lead you on.

Sometimes, like now, sitting here I feel very warm and I wish you were here. Nick, my prayer is you will get out without me making a decision. I have not, up until now, felt pity or pressure, but Nick, my question is do I go solely on what *you* feel, and then my feelings will grow very strong and very intense?

Oh, Greek, I'm sorry I'm so stubborn or whatever, but I guess I'm looking at *every* angle that ever was 'cause I sure don't want to make a mistake. I just wish you were here to hold me and I would know how I feel. But then again, I would probably think it was my flesh taking over 'cause of neat feelings — like flesh! (I want feelings, but then I wouldn't trust them either!)

Sir, you sure did pick or open yourself up to a stupid, mixed-up little girl. I'm sorry, but with Jesus' help, I'll get it together. I do love you and care *very* much what happens to you. When I'm away and think of all you say, I think my feelings are stronger. Maybe that room [visiting room in prison] just isn't the place. Maybe I'm just a brat!

Nick, all I'm going on right now is, you can't be wrong. If you feel this is right and your love is meant only for me, then God is faithful. Are you for sure and certain there is *no* doubt God means us to be together? If He does, then for sure I have to be there. Fact, faith, feeling. It is so opposite the world's way. Nick, if I ever married you and then had doubts, I don't know how I'd handle them. I think I'd rather be dead than have that happen. I really ask God that you be out, and we have time together before He asks me to make a commitment. . . .

I'm real sleepy so good night and tell your celly he's lucky he's not mixed up with me. I feel bad for you! But I'm trying to learn to listen.

Love,
Dottie

Hi there Teach!

Wow, I praise the Lord for your letter! You made me feel like singing, and I did. I sang praises to our Lord Jesus and for your feelings and your words. . . .

I wish I could be with you right this moment. You'd have a very hard time getting out of my hug. Smile! I am also very happy to hear that you trust me and that you believe me. Also, I am very blessed to hear that you see that our meeting, our love, our everything is from above. I wish that we were together and to ourselves and had time so we can empty our hearts out to each other. . . .

I didn't have any intention of falling in love with anyone but I told you how I felt when I met you.

Our love is blessed from above. We do care and love one another, and we are led with His divine hands. You feel comfortable close to me, don't you? Our love is true and real. I will try to never make you sad or sorry that we have gotten it together. I speak as a man to his woman. And one more thing for sure: We won't have to worry or feel blue because Christ is staying in first place in both of our lives. Amen!

Nick

Good Evening Nick,

I'm home alone right now and I'm missing you. I'm listening to the "Wedding Song" by Paul Stookey — "Woman draws her life from man and gives it back again" — "If loving is the answer, then who's it given for?" Those are a couple of lines. It begins, "Union of our spirits has caused you to remain." If ya' come, I'll let ya' hear it. O.K.? Oh, by the way, I like "Moon River" a lot. . . .

Nick, you love Christ so much and so many people look up to you and yet you see something special in me. I do know why and yet I don't. I for sure love God and trust Him, but I'm not strong in faith or even "guts" like you are. I want to do things for you and share with you all I've learned about living and loving from Him. But I *really* don't know much. I don't know what you could have learned from me except love is *patient* and also the idea of gentleness probably came across. I'm very glad you love me, and I know I'll grow as He leads. But — Wow! — the idea of how much you care about me is very hard for me to realize in my head.

So Nikos! As of now, I can say I love you. I want to be with you and learn with you and from you. I really would feel more assurance handling hard times if you were there. . . .

The thought of how much you love me amazes me,

and for the first time I'm getting excited to just be with you. Not just looking forward to sharing Christ with you, but I actually want to be with you. . . . I just thank Him as I write these things. I feel peaceful and good.

I'm also aware of the time we're living in, and I know you are going to be one of the leaders for Him. I know this probably will be heavy — I don't know how heavy, and I also know I can't make it on my own. Only on His strength will I make it, and I prefer to make it on His strength in both of us, by your side.

Well goodnight, love,
Dottie

Good evening there, sweet girl!

Praise God for the sweetest girl in this world! Honey, I pray that my letter finds my Bestest Friend in His peace, and resting in His divine love — Dottie Elliott I love you!

Honey, I like for you to know that I was in prayer all day long for you, for me, for *us* and all our loved ones. I gave praise and thanks to our Lord for leading to me the sweetest girl in the world, and for the prettiest girl in the world! I asked our Lord to please watch over you and lead us for His name sake and glory. Honey, I believe one day real soon we are to be together, and forever. Hey girl! We are meant to be, and we together will meet whatever is ahead of our lives. Right? Right!

Hey, before I forget, Cullen showed me a few pages of a magazine that has rings in it. Susan sent it to him, and I like some of the rings. Can you find out from Susan what address or where is the store? . . .

Sa agapo para pali, girl!
Nickey

Dear Nick,

I wrote these [vows] when I was thinking of us after I wrote that letter about being together:

"I give myself to you today, Nick, to be your wife. I'll be your helpmate and walk with you and support you with the strength given by our God.

"I respect you and trust you and I will take your word as *truth* as coming from Him and I will submit to your leadership as I do to Christ. For you are to love me as Christ loved the church and just as He was given charge of His body, the church, so are you in charge of me.

"I will love you and care for you and together we will be a channel through which the Living God can love.

"I *am* my beloved's."

Dottie

Satan
Strikes Back!

One of the first principles I learned as a Christian is that reaching a spiritual peak always opens you up to more intense attacks from Satan.

Falling in love with Dottie and then having her return my love was a spiritual peak for me. God had heard my prayers for a Christian wife and had answered them in the most magnificent way. I was on top of the world! But I was also extremely vulnerable to Satan's retaliation because my guard was down. It was like what happened sometimes when I used to get in fights on the street. I might get in a good punch or knife thrust and then relax a little, thinking I'd won the battle. But that was the moment I found I needed to be the most careful because if my blow hadn't finished off my opponent, the chances were he would counterattack in such a superhuman rage that I might actually end up losing.

As you know, I believed in Satan before I committed my life to Christ. I even followed Satan and regarded myself as his "son-in-law." I kept on believing in Satan after becoming a Christian, but I don't think I had any idea how my former allegiance to the evil one could apparently make him even more intent on working me over. I know a lot of Christian believers who have problems with Satan that are relatively subtle. He often strikes when they are on some kind of "spiritual high," after God has done something great in their lives. But he tempts them and trips them up and "knifes" them in ways that are sometimes hard to understand or even see at first.

But it wasn't like that with me. When Satan came after me, there could be no mistake about what was happening. He might try to nudge some people off the right road with a slight bit of pressure on their "steering wheels." But with me, it was like he was trying to run over me head-on with a Mack truck.

Let me give you a concrete example. At about the time things really started to go well with Dottie and me, I started getting some flak from inmates who were known Satan-worshipers. Like I said, there wasn't going to be anything subtle for me as far as Satan was concerned. On one Saturday night, I was waiting on a catwalk for the guard to open my cell so I could go in for the night, when this guy named Tony, who was into astroprojection and witchcraft, sneaked up behind me and plucked a hair out of my head.

"Tonight, Greek!" he said. "Tonight is your night. You're going to get it. The hex is on you."

"Whatever you do to me, double back to you in the name of the Lord Jesus Christ!" I said.

I went on into my cell and didn't think much more about Tony. My celly, a guy named Hogan, got in just as they were turning the lights out for the night, and I decided to go right to bed instead of reading by candlelight, because my eyes felt kind of heavy.

I fell asleep almost immediately and started to dream this strange dream. At first, I thought I was in a church service because I was in this sanctuary-type room with a bunch of people who were standing around chanting and bowing their heads. Many of the people were wearing monk-like robes, held together by a rope around the waist.

I thought, "Wow, this is beautiful!" and I settled down to enjoy the service. The leader of the group, a tall guy who was wearing one of the cassocks, moved up to the altar and opened a huge book that was resting on a stand. I couldn't see his face because it was mostly covered by a hood over his head, but his voice came out rich and forceful as he said, "The text today is a familiar one. It concerns Jesus of Nazareth." Then he began to read, "The Virgin Mary was a whore and Jesus Christ was a bastard. . . ."

"Hold on!" I interrupted. "That's a lie! You know he's the Son of God! You're misquoting Scripture. The Bible says a virgin shall bear a son and his name shall be Immanuel, God among us."

"Quiet! You're out of order!" he said, raising his head so I could see his face. He was a handsome, forceful-looking man except for one thing — his eyes. They were so glassy they didn't look human. He looked like he was totally doped up on cocaine or some other drug, except that he was too much in control of himself to be any drug addict.

"Oh, oh!" I said. "I know what I'm under now. I rebuke you in the name of Jesus! I'm washed in the blood of the Lamb, and you're a liar. I'm bought by a price, and you're a liar. The Bible says you're going to be cast into the bottomless pit. Aren't you the one that made nations quake? Aren't you the one that made kings shake? Greater is he that is in me than he that is in you!"

By this time, this demon, who was maybe Satan himself, was really angry at me. And as some of his fellow worshipers looked up during the argument and I saw their faces, I recognized at least one — my relative who had practiced witchcraft in Greece. She looked a little older than when I had known her as a kid, but she was apparently into the same kind of tricks.

The leader started calling Jesus and his disciples homosexuals and made all sorts of other wild accusations, and I waded right in defending the true identity of Christ by using Scripture. But the intensity of the evil in that room was so overwhelming, I finally started panting and found I couldn't take it any more. That was when I woke up, drenched in sweat. The cell was pitch black, and I knew I was really in my own little corner of the prison and not in a Satan worshiper's sanctuary, But for some reason, that didn't end the thing. I could still hear the chanting, and even though my eyes were wide open, I could see those people dancing around their leader.

I knew now I had to rely on more than my own spiritual powers and my memory of Scripture. So I hopped out of bed, grabbed my Bible and knelt down on the floor and started trying to light a candle I kept in the cell. As I was fumbling around, my celly, Hogan, sat up in his bunk, looked over at me, and said, "What the. . . ." and passed right out.

With the candle flickering in front of me, I started reading out loud, directly from the Bible, and I punctuated those readings with hurried renditions of the Lord's Prayer: "OurFatherwhoartinheavenhallowedbethyname. . . ." And I said, "Get behind me, Satan—I bind you in the name of Jesus!"

I was trembling and sweating when I started this routine at about 3:20 in the morning, and when I finally got some peace it was about 5:00 A.M. When the bugle blew later that morning and I got up to prepare for church, I was still shaking a little, and a couple of guys commented on how pale my face was.

My celly waked up soon after I did and the first

thing he said was, "What was going on last night? I felt the presence of evil and I heard music and chanting. At one point, I almost felt like I got knocked out."

I was pretty sure that my experience had been more than a dream, and this seemed to confirm it. But because I still wasn't completely sure about what had happened, I pulled Rev. Sorg aside after the church service and said, "Don't think I'm being crazy, but something happened to me last night. . . ." And I told him every detail of the story.

"God has his hand on you and will take care of you," Sorg said. "But if God wants to use you, it's not unusual for Satan to show you things that he hopes will scare you. He wants you to stop your work."

Then he told me the story of Daniel. Sorg said, "Daniel had to go through a living hell just as you did, except it lasted for twenty-one days." This was while the mighty evil spirit that ruled the kingdom of Persia blocked the way of God's messenger.

This was one reason I loved Sorg so much: he often gave me greater spiritual perspective on problems I was facing. And in this case, he assured me I wasn't losing my mind. This was the first time I had engaged in spiritual warfare and successfully withstood satanic attacks as one of God's soldiers. So you can imagine how scary the whole thing was for me.

But that's not the end of the story. When I was walking from the chapel service to get my lunch, I ran into Tony, the Satan worshiper, and three of his buddies. And they looked terrible. They were all marked up, with bruises, cuts, and scratches on their arms and faces, and they looked like they had been on the losing end of a gang fight.

"Man, what happened to you guys?" I asked.

It seemed they had run into a spiritual battle themselves the previous night. Something like a hurricane had hit their cell, even though all the windows were closed. Their books and other objects on shelves had started to fly down around them and some candles they were using for the Satan ceremony had almost caused a fire. Their toilet had backed up on them, and they had had to spend most of the morning cleaning things up. The mess their room was in was especially upsetting to them because they had one of the best-equipped rooms in the entire prison.

My skin was crawling as they told me what had happened, and I was just happy I had been on the right side of that spiritual battle. But I knew this was only the first skirmish in an ongoing war that would engage much of my energy during my stay in prison. I had been Satan's right-hand man in my little criminal circle in Cleveland, but now I was even more active in opposing him through the prison ministry we had developed. It was only natural that he would try to put me down and discourage me every time he got a chance.

Some of these put-downs and discouragements may not have been quite as dramatic as that spiritual battle in my cell, but they were often more devastating to my morale. One of the main problems of this type that I faced involved my status as an immigrant. This issue would probably never have become important if I had been content to be an ordinary inmate until my time was up and I was released. But I wanted honor-farm status, so I could get a temporary leave from prison—called "institutional bond"—and go out into the community outside the prison to preach and give my testimony.

The chaplains had arranged for a number of the most reliable inmates to make outside trips on this institutional bond, and I saw no reason I shouldn't be granted the privilege too. Besides, I was so enthusiastic about my faith and ministry, I wanted outsiders to know what we were doing, so they could see that Jesus was alive and well behind bars.

But because I had been born in Greece, I had to write a letter to the immigration authorities to get a statement saying I didn't have any detainers on me or any black marks against me as an immigrant. So I wrote a letter, but I didn't get quite the answer I was expecting. They notified me that they would have to have a hearing on my case in prison and that I would be notified about the date of the meeting. But there was never any notification. I was just called out of my chaplain's job one day and ushered right into a hearing.

Five stern-looking officials were staring at me from behind a long table covered with papers which apparently related to my case.

"You're going to have a deportation hearing at this time, Mr. Pirovolos," the head guy on this board told me. "Do you understand English?"

"Some," I said, but I hadn't quite figured out what this was all about. A deportation hearing? I didn't want to get deported—I just wanted institutional bond so I could preach the gospel!

"We have evidence that your brother is a Communist, your father is—"

"That's not true!" I interrupted.

"Also, you've committed many crimes in this country, so you've committed acts of moral turpitude. . . ."

I don't know how long I stood there listening to them list all the things I or my family had supposedly done wrong. Some of it was true, some of it was totally false. But the upshot was they told me I couldn't get institutional bond like all the other guys, and I was also being scheduled to be deported from the United States.

That hurt. It hurt because I thought I was doing

what God wanted me to do, and now it seemed I was to be punished even more. It hurt because I had already started developing a relationship with Dottie when this problem arose, and I wondered, what's to happen now? Am I to be separated by an ocean from the only girl I've ever really loved?

But the thing that hurt most of all was the reaction of some of the other inmates. Guys who had always seemed fairly friendly started making fun of me. They said, "Hey, Greek, where's your God now?" There was nothing I could say to them in response. I knew God hadn't deserted me, but I was in a tough position. What, I wondered, was God doing with me?

So to try to find out, I fell right down on my knees when I returned to my cell and I prayed, "God, I don't mind going back to Greece. But I really want to stay here. My family is here. I've lived more than half my life here. But if you want me to go there, I know you're there as much as you're here. Please help me, and if you can drop my deportation —*even on the very last day of my stay in prison* — I'd be indebted to you, God."

But I didn't get an answer right away. In fact, things went from bad to worse. As Dottie and I got more deeply involved with each other, she started trying to help me out with the immigration people. But after we had decided to get married, they told her our marriage wouldn't do a thing to stop the deportation.

They even started threatening to deport her as well as me if we got married. I don't know if they could legally have done that, but that's the kind of pressure I was operating under for nearly two years while I was in prison.

Dottie wouldn't give up, though. She kept trying to straighten out the immigration thing, and she also worked to get me paroled. She tried everybody, from the governor of Ohio on down, and she kept getting advice to hire this one lawyer who was supposed to have counseled thousands of inmates and was said to have some influence with parole officials. I was willing to try almost anything at that point because I had just had as bad an experience with my first parole hearing as I'd had with the deportation people.

I was up for parole about a year after my deportation hearing, and I was fairly optimistic about my chances. I had developed a good reputation for my coffeehouse ministry, and many of the guards and chaplains were behind me. But with this parole board, that didn't make a bit of difference.

The two men sitting on the parole board started in on me just like the immigration officials had done: "Your brother is a Communist. Why did you come to America? Why didn't you stay in Greece?" Not only that, they cursed at me and called my mother and grandmother filthy names.

I could feel my temper rising, but I held it in check. I should say, *God* held it in check. It was only by the grace of God's Spirit that I was able to keep a level head in that hearing.

"What is this born-again stuff, this business about Nick the Greek in the coffeehouse?" one of the men asked.

"Jesus Christ changed my life," I said. "I know he can be an answer for criminals in our society, and I want to continue to work with prison inmates when I get out of here."

One of the officials softened a little at this, and he said, "In some ways, you've done a good job here, and the institution is proud of you for that. But we can't overlook what you've done. You should have found God twenty years ago. So we're going to give you another forty-five months to think about it. Now, get out of here."

"God bless you, and have a nice Easter," I said — and I meant it. I wasn't being sarcastic.

But once again, I had to face the guards and inmates who were waiting to see how the hearing had gone. Many of them were optimistic about my chances for parole, and several put their thumbs up as I walked out and asked, "Greek, you got it, didn't you?"

But I put my thumbs down and went on back to my cell again. Others then started asking that same question I was getting used to hearing now: "Where's your God now, Greek?"

And I had to tell them I didn't know exactly why God didn't want me out. Maybe if I had been released then, I would have been deported back to Greece right away. Maybe God wanted to protect me by keeping me in prison. But I didn't know, and I'll freely admit, it was frustrating, having to wait and wait to see how everything would finally turn out.

Despite the discomfort I was experiencing, I know now this was an important time of spiritual growth for me. God was allowing me to face these trials and fears, to engage in hand-to-hand combat with Satan, because I had a lot to learn about trusting him and waiting for him to act in his time on my behalf. I couldn't see where all this was leading. For all I knew, I would end up in Greece, far away from the people I loved and the ministry I had assumed God was arranging for me. None of it made any sense. But gradually, I learned to watch and wait as I prayed and prayed for months and, finally, years for these things to be completely resolved.

Part of the testing and learning involved some spiritual training in how to combat Satan's attacks even when I was in a relatively weakened condition. I desperately wanted to get out of prison even at the same time I wanted to do God's will. The danger was that I would start to rationalize and convince myself that it *had* to be God's will that I be released from prison — and be released as soon as possible — when that might not be his will at all. And if I assumed that it was definitely his will that I get out right away, I would be highly susceptible to trying to use any means at my disposal to be released, even if those means were not quite honest.

It was at this point that the lawyer who was supposed to be the best in getting parole boards to listen to inmates' pleas came to us. He had supposedly counseled thousands of prisoners and had a reputation for getting a lot of them released. So someone got this lawyer to set up a meeting to talk things over.

But it became apparent in the first few minutes of our conversation that something was terribly wrong with this man. He said, "I think I can take care of your case fairly easily, but I'll need some extra money. Some of the people I know expect a few good lunches out of this, and there are some other personal payments, if you know what I mean. . . ."

"No way!" I said. "I'd rather never breathe free air again than compromise. You get out of here with your bag of tricks! If you don't leave this room right now, I will personally body-slam you to the ground. You expect me to stick my finger in God's eye? Is that what you want me to do?"

I must have looked like a crazy man; I wasn't dressed well, since I had been dragged out of a shower into this meeting without any prior warning. I wasn't wearing any socks, and my shirt was soaking wet because I hadn't even had time to dry myself off.

"But I know the governor!" he said. "I can get you out of here!"

"It sounds to me like you got too much 'I' trouble. Now get out!" And as I started moving toward him, he beat a quick exit.

He then contacted Dottie and explained he had met me, but that I was quite fanatical—and perhaps *she* could see things more clearly. But she said, "I'm afraid my answer is the same, sir! Money is always available, but not for this type of game. So you leave him alone!"

I was glad to have Dottie on my side. She was even starting to talk like me. But sometimes I got the feeling Dottie was the *only* one on my side—that is, Dottie and God and maybe a couple of the prison chaplains. The odds seemed overwhelmingly against me. It didn't look like I'd get out of prison while I was still a young man. And if I did get out, my chances seemed even worse for staying in this country. I knew I was involved in some sort of serious spiritual warfare, but I couldn't figure out exactly where the front lines were. I knew Satan was putting it to me, but I couldn't see where it was all leading. I was sure God wanted me to do his will, but it wasn't so clear to me what his will was.

It was all especially hard on Dottie. She had told me of her love and vowed to marry me. But for all she knew, I might never be paroled, and that meant I'd have to stay in prison until 1996. And if I did manage to get out, the immigration people might send me right back to Greece. Not a very bright outlook for love and marriage, but that was what she faced. Or maybe I should say, that was *part* of what she faced. She still had to tell her family about me, but what was she supposed to say? I could just hear her telling her father, "Uh, Dad, there's this Greek I want to marry, but there are a couple of things about him. He's a convict, he's cut people up and robbed them, and he's being deported back to Greece. . . ."

I wasn't exactly the kind of guy I would have wanted *my* daughter to marry. So how could I expect any different attitude in Dottie's folks?

But that's the way God works sometimes. He lets us walk along in a fog so we can't see what's ahead of us. Not only that, he sometimes makes us teeter in that fog on the edge of a thousand-foot cliff. I think that's what the Bible means when it says we "walk by faith, not by sight" in 2 Corinthians 5:7. God puts us in situations where it seems like we're in an impossible trap. There's nothing we can do by our own power to escape, and all that's left is to trust him. And that's when *we* start to learn what the Apostle Paul learned in 2 Corinthians 12:9 where God said to him, "My grace is sufficient for you, for my power is made perfect in weakness."

Clearly, I was at the end of my rope. Now it was all up to God. All he wanted was for me to recognize that fact. So I prayed. And Dottie prayed. And all our Christian friends, inside and outside prison, prayed. And God listened to us, and he acted. Here's how he eventually responded to our prayers so dramatically it made my head spin:

Dottie's family accepted me with open arms. Her grandfather, who was the "chief" of their clan, was the one she thought would take the news hardest. But when she asked him, "Granddad, what do you think?" he responded by writing a letter of welcome to me. And her dad said, "You haven't given us anything to doubt about you in twenty-six years. Why should we start now?"

Deportation proceedings against me were dropped on November 1, 1974. It took about a year and a half of wading through a lot of paperwork and red tape. Also, we contacted thousands — yes, literally *thousands* — of friends and fellow believers to write letters on my behalf. But when the hearing was finally opened, I showed up with five lawyers who had volunteered to represent me, and I had thousands of letters from fellow inmates and former inmates who said,

"There will be injustice for Nick the Greek if he is deported."

The judge was impressed, but he said, "If the immigration people show up to contest this case, there may be a tough argument against you. But if they don't show up, you can have the charges against you dropped and they can't reopen the case." The message I got was clear: I just prayed they wouldn't show up.

It looked like I'd make it — up until the very last minute. But just as the judge prepared to hand down his decision, we all heard footsteps hurrying toward us from the back of the courtroom. I thought, "Oh, no, Lord, it's the immigration people!"

But it wasn't. It was Congressman James Stanton of Ohio and one of his colleagues rushing in to contribute more testimony and letters on my behalf. So the judge found me innocent of all charges. I don't pretend to know exactly how this was all done. I just know that God did it. But I should mention one final thing about this hearing: Even though deportation proceedings against me were dropped, nothing was said about a detainer or holder that the immigration authorities had put on me a couple of years before, just to be sure I'd be around if they wanted to ship me back to Greece. Did the existence of that holder mean I might still get deported, despite the judge's decision? I didn't know, and wouldn't find out until a few months later. But I didn't worry too much about it then because I was too happy. The deportation decision meant I now could qualify for institutional bond. In other words, I could go out on temporary leave to fulfill speaking assignments, and as a result, I would have more opportunities to see Dottie.

I got married to Dottie on January 30, 1975, while I was still an inmate. This may seem too matter-of-fact, the way I put this. But you've got to understand,

God was answering prayers so fast—boom! boom! boom!—that I hardly had time to adjust to one great thing before the next came along.

And the wedding really was a fast-and-furious affair. We were supposed to get married a week later, while I was out on an institutional bond assignment, and plans were being made to fit me for a tux and have quite a few people attend. There was even talk of TV coverage. After all, it wasn't just every day that a crook-turned-Christian-prison-evangelist gets a day out from behind bars to tie the knot.

But it didn't work quite like we planned. Governor Rhodes of Ohio had just gone into office and decided he was going to restrict the right of inmates to go out on temporary leave. This meant I couldn't plan on the date we had set. But it would be a few days before the governor's order went into effect, so if we wanted to get married, we'd have to act immediately or put off the ceremony indefinitely.

I decided to act. Father George Koerber, the Catholic chaplain at Mansfield, agreed to marry us. But there was no time to make any advance preparations. In fact, I didn't even have time to tell Dottie what I was planning. As a matter of fact, I didn't even know the exact day. I knew we had to act fast, and I told the priest what I wanted to do. But then I left it up to him to choose the date.

On January 30, I had an outside speaking assignment. As we got into the chaplain's car that day, he said, "We're not going to the speaking engagement."

"Where are we going?" I said.

"You're getting married today."

I didn't say anything at first to that, so he asked, "Can I persuade you to get married today?"

"Whatever you think," I said. But he knew I was turning cartwheels inside.

Things happened so fast after that, I still have trouble sorting it all out. I called some friends of mine and Dottie's — we called them "Mom" and "Pop" Uvegas — and I told them to meet us right away. Mrs. Uvegas came in with her hair still wet from a shampoo at the beauty shop where we had called her, and she said, "What's happening?"

"We're going to have a wedding today," I said.

"Does Dottie know?" she asked.

"No, not yet," I said.

"You'd better call her. She's still in school."

So I called her school and asked the principal if I could talk with her. When she got on the phone, I still didn't mention the wedding. I just said, "Meet me at the Uvegases' house."

"What's wrong?" she asked.

"Nothing's wrong. I just want to talk with you."

Maybe I should have told her right out, but I didn't want to shock her. I wanted to talk with her in person. Meanwhile, Father Koerber was running around trying to find a Catholic church. He found a big one near the apartment house where we were waiting and managed to talk the priest into helping us out. By the time Dottie arrived, we had almost everything planned — the church, a wedding cake, even our rings, which had just happened to come into the jewelry store that day.

I met Dottie downstairs in a parking lot and said, "You know, honey, the wedding is changed."

"Oh," she said. "Maybe two weeks later?"

"No, the wedding is for today. Is that okay with you?"

She was wearing a casual pantsuit and I was standing there in my prison blues, and I knew she was wondering how we could get married looking like that. But she hardly blinked an eye. "That's all right," she said. "My father and brother will love this because it will have to be a small wedding. And they

194

didn't want to wear a tux anyway.''

So it was settled, and before I knew it, I was standing in that Catholic chapel, with Father Koerber conducting the wedding ceremony in an oversized robe that the local priest had lent him. There were supposed to be hundreds of people there, but we had only twelve. My own mother hadn't even been able to make it because of the short notice. But when I told Dottie my vows, I meant them like nothing I'd ever meant in my whole life.

Just as the priest pronounced us "man and wife," the chimes of the church started ringing all over the place, because it had just turned six o'clock. That really gave me goose pimples because I knew God was saying, "I'm here, blessing this marriage."

Then we went back to the Uvegases' place and had some Kentucky Fried Chicken Father Koerber bought for us and the top layer of a wedding cake the Uvegas family had saved for their daughter's first anniversary. We ate and talked, and before I left, Dottie and I stepped into the next room, kissed good-bye, and that was our honeymoon. By 9:00 P.M. I was back in my cell, showing my wedding ring to my celly. I couldn't sleep all night; I was thinking about what had happened that day. Dottie came to visit me the next morning, and she was wearing the dress she was supposed to have worn on our real honeymoon. I'll never forget it. It was a green polka-dot dress, and we spent almost the whole visiting period just hugging each other.

Now I knew I could make it. Even if I had to stay in prison for years longer, I could still make it because I had somebody who loved me waiting for me. You don't know what it means, to have somebody waiting for you.

I went before the parole board again on February 11, 1975. Just before I went in for this hearing, I was reading about the parable of the talents in Matthew

25 — how those servants who had used their talents wisely were rewarded, and how the slothful servant was punished. I don't know why I was reading that particular passage because I had read it a thousand times before, and I forgot about it when I walked up before the two hearing officers.

This time, the whole atmosphere was different. They didn't make accusations against my brothers and my father. Instead, they wanted me to tell them about how I had almost gotten into trouble over the keys to the coffeehouse. But instead of being stern with me, they laughed through the whole story. Then one of the officers, a woman, glanced at my ring finger and asked, "When did that happen?"

When I told her all about it, she said, "I'm so happy for you, Nick." Then she told me to step outside so they could come to a decision. I couldn't figure out what was happening. The parole board actually seemed friendly for once. But I was still nervous and I wasn't expecting much. I had no reason to expect much, in light of what had happened to me in the past.

Then I heard the buzzer that meant I was supposed to come back in. The woman on the board didn't beat around the bush. She said, "We have decided to recommend parole."

And I started to cry. I said, "Look at what I was reading before I came in here," and I pulled out my Bible and showed them the parable of the talents. "What the Lord is saying to me is, 'Nick, you go out there and use your talents!' " And that woman parole officer started crying with me.

When I walked back outside into the hallway, everything was different than before. I raised my thumbs skyward this time, and I shouted, "Praise God!" This time, the guards and inmates waiting around there were with me. They shouted and clapped their hands and congratulated me, and I kept on praising God for what he was doing in my life.

But the tension wasn't over yet. My release date was set for March 14, 1975. But the nearer the day drew, the more worried I got about that holder the immigration authorities still had on me. I knew I had won at the deportation hearing. But I also knew the American government bureaucracy well enough to know that the left hand might not know what the right hand was doing. In other words, I might have been found innocent of all charges by that deportation judge, but some obscure immigration official might still be guided by that holder. And before I knew it, I could find myself back in Greece — and then what would I do?

So I grew more and more uncomfortable as the day of my release approached. I thought it would be okay, but I wasn't sure. And that uncertainty can make life miserable, especially if you're marking time in a cell and are relatively powerless to take any action on your own. Sure, I had people like Dottie and other friends looking into the matter for me. But they couldn't seem to come up with any definite answers.

Then on March 14, as I was preparing to leave the prison, I heard my name being announced over the public address system. "83284, report to the deputy's office!" the voice said.

I figured that was it. It was all a hoax. "You ain't going nowhere," I told myself. "They're just playing with your head!"

But when I reached the deputy's office, I was handed a letter showing that my deportation detainer had been dropped. And then I remembered. I had prayed two years before for God to take care of this deportation problem for me — *even if it was on the very last day of my prison term*. And that's exactly what he had done!

So now, there was nothing left for me to do but leave. But I was scared. In a funny way, I didn't want to leave. I had spent four years of my life in a cell, and I didn't know what the real world was like anymore. Sure, I had been out a few times in the last couple of months on institutional bond. But that was just for a day at a time. In those cases, I was still a prisoner, and I knew I was a prisoner. Now I couldn't remember how to drive a car. I was afraid of people. I suspected they wouldn't accept an ex-convict. I was also afraid I might fail and go back into my old way of life. I knew I was a Christian, but I was also a weak human being, and I hadn't been tested in the outside world as a believer. Would my faith be strong enough to sustain me?

So it was a long walk from the deputy's office through the release procedures and finally out into the open air. I was wearing a tan suit they had given me, and the shoes Dottie had sent in for release day didn't fit. As I walked toward the spot where Dottie was supposed to pick me up, somebody switched on the loudspeaker system and said, "Hey, Greek, take care! God be with you. 83284, we wish you the best!" And hundreds of guys started banging their cups against the bars to wish me farewell.

Snow was falling when I walked outside, and ice on the walkway made it hard to keep my balance. But I didn't care because I saw Dottie standing out there in the snow, beside her little Maverick. We hugged and kissed, but before we left, we stopped and thanked the Lord that I was out, once and for all.

But then I said, "Let's get away from here before they change their minds." And before I knew it, we were on the freeway, speeding toward an entirely new life—one which would in many ways be more demanding than the one I had faced behind bars.

The Return
of the Greek

Being outside a prison isn't necessarily the same thing as being free. As I told you before, I was always looking for freedom when I was a "free man," but I never found it. I had to get behind bars before I really discovered what true liberty means.

It was the same kind of thing when I was released from prison. I realized I was free, not because I was on the outside now, but because Jesus Christ had taken over my *inner* life and given me the only kind of personal freedom that really means anything. In fact, I found in some ways I was less free in an external sense because I wasn't sure exactly who I was or what I was supposed to do. I knew I was a child of God, but what did that mean in terms of my work and ministry? I had understood what my mission was with the coffeehouse and other evangelistic outreaches in prison. But now, my specific calling in life wasn't so clear.

One thing I did know was that I wanted to work with people in the garbage world, the criminals and prisoners whose way of life I understood so well because I had been there myself. But how to go about it? That was my problem.

Dottie suggested that I just relax for a couple of months, but I couldn't do that. I wanted to get started. So I started doing some counseling with delinquent kids and I also did some speaking to community groups about how they could help those in prison. But I was still trying to find my way, and God didn't seem to be giving me any clear signals.

But then shortly after my release from prison, I had a dream. Actually, it wasn't really a dream, because I wasn't asleep. It was more of a vision. I had just come home from a speaking assignment in a local prison, and I was dead tired. Dottie was in the kitchen preparing our food, and I said, "Honey, I'm going to take a little nap. When I wake up, I'll take a shower, eat, and go to bed."

But as soon as I lay down on the couch, my mind started to drift in a definite direction, a direction over which I was exercising no control myself. The scene I saw in my mind's eye was a beautiful meadow with scores and scores of sheep jumping around, as though they were real happy. They were bleating and seemed to be having a lot of fun running about—except for one thing. Every so often, a hand would reach out of the corner of the picture, grab one of the sheep by an ear, and slit its throat. As the mortally wounded sheep bled and kicked, it was put on a pile with other dead and dying sheep.

The second time this hand reached out, I followed it to its source. First, I saw the shoulder, then the neck, and then the face of the person who was doing this terrible thing. And as I looked into his glassy eyes and rather handsome face, I realized it was the same man, the demonic monk, who had been leading those Satan worshipers in my violent dream in prison.

This guy half-smiled at me in an evil way and then

went on about his business of killing the sheep. I was so terrified, I screamed, "Dottie! Dottie!"

She came right to my side and asked, "What's wrong! What's wrong, Nick?" But I motioned to her to wait beside me until the vision was finished. So she sat there and prayed for me because she knew I was going through a heavy thing.

With my eyes closed, I watched the living sheep jumping around as their brothers and sisters and friends were being slaughtered.

So I asked, "What's wrong with those sheep? Don't they see what's happening to their fellow sheep?"

And then a voice told me, "Take a look at their eyes."

So I looked at their eyes and I saw cataracts, thick cloudy shields on each of their eyes. "What does this mean?" I asked. And as I was waiting for an answer, the killing continued, and I could hardly stand it. Dottie was holding on to me, and I wanted her to hold the sheep so I could go after the guy who was killing them and box his ears. I had hate for this man who was killing those sheep for no reason.

I asked God, "Lord, what does this mean?"

And he gave this interpretation: "The sheep are like children. I have made them all equal. They are all my children. The hand you saw reaching out is the devil, who wants to devour as many as he can. The cataracts you saw in the eyes of the sheep jumping and running around represent the blindness in the hearts of many church people. They run around saying, 'Praise God this isn't happening to me.' But they could care less that their brothers and sisters are dying right and left. They are hung up on their own little denominational backgrounds, their circles of friends and their own personal concerns. But they lack the insight to see what's really happening all around them."

"But what can I do?" I asked.

"I want you to be my spokesman," the Lord said. "I want you to show those blind sheep how to get those cataracts out of their eyes."

Now, I understood. I knew plenty of people, church members and those outside the churches, who really had no feel for the pain many of their less fortunate neighbors were going through. They saw a juvenile delinquent or a drug addict or a convict, and they just said, "That's too bad. But there's nothing *I* can do about their problems, so I'll just tend to my own business and enjoy the blessings God has given me."

But I could never be satisfied with that attitude, and God knew it. I guess that was why he tapped me to see this vision, because he knew I'd be likely to act on it. And he also knew I had some experience with this glassy-eyed guy who was killing the sheep. The devil was an old acquaintance of mine, and I knew better than many people just how dangerous he was.

In case I was inclined to forget about the power of evil in this world, I had plenty of reminders in my first few weeks outside prison. You see, a lot of my old friends and colleagues in the garbage world didn't really believe I had gone straight. They either wanted me to join in with them again, or they were so afraid of me and what I knew about them, they wanted to rub me out. As I had expected, it wasn't so easy just to ignore my old way of life after I walked past those prison walls back into the real world.

Just a few days after I was released, for example, I ran into one of my old bosses. At one point in my first year in prison, his nephew had offered to put up $50,000 to bribe somebody to get me out, but it wasn't accepted. God truly had built a wall around me, and no man could open the door until God so granted. But I guess this guy still didn't really believe I had changed my ways. Dottie was with me when I met him, and almost before I could get a word out of my mouth, he had pulled $7000 out of his pocket and said, "Here, go buy some furniture, then take a week off and come back to work for me."

There was no question in my mind or in Dottie's. It was just like the deal the lawyer in prison had offered. It was not of God. So I said, "Don't you know what's happened in my life? Don't you know Jesus Christ has come into my life?"

He didn't really understand. But he did put that $7000 back in his pocket. Some of my encounters with my old underworld connections weren't so easy to handle, though. In fact, there were enough threats over the phone that Dottie and I arranged for me to call her every two hours while I was away from her so that she could go directly to some key friends and finally to the police and get them involved right at the outset if I seemed to have disappeared.

This warning system was almost used one day after I had been out of prison for about a month. Three guys I had known from one of the Cleveland mobs cornered me and made me go into the back of a little bar, where they threatened to cut me into little pieces and feed me to the fish in Lake Erie.

"We'd like to waste you, you know," one of the guys said. "You open your guts on anything about us, and you're finished."

I chuckled at that, and I think that took them off guard. "You gonna feed me to the fish?" I said. "Okay, so now they'll have more to eat than before because I'm getting chubbier."

Those guys didn't know what to say to that because I guess I didn't seem scared. So I started witnessing to them about Jesus. I said, "Hey, man, did you see what happened in my life? Jesus Christ came into my life! He set me free. I rebuke you in the name of Jesus!"

They looked at me like I'd flipped out. But I kept on: "Greater is he that is in me than he that is in you! I'm washed in the blood of the Lamb—and you should try it too!"

"Yeah, good for you but not good for me," one of the guys finally said. Even though they weren't convinced by what I was saying, they didn't talk about trying to cut me up after that. But they did keep me past the time when I was supposed to check in by phone with Dottie. She was beside herself with worry and had already started putting through some emergency calls when I finally got in touch with her.

Occasionally, I'd run into guys who were even more dangerous. They liked to shoot first, and *maybe* speak later. I was driving home one night in a van, and this little Chevy passed me right in the middle of a bridge, and somebody in the car started shooting. The whole van began to shake, and I was sure I had been shot in the stomach. The driver took off real fast so I couldn't tell who it was, and I stopped and checked myself and the van real close but I didn't find any bullet holes.

Things like this made me much more confident in the ability of God to guide me through the thickets of the outside, non-prison world that I had been so afraid would snare me in my old way of life. I guess I should have known God had the power to sustain me. And one part of me did know. But I don't think you ever know or understand completely how God works in a given situation until you walk through the fire of experience.

For example, if you had told me, while I was sitting in my little cell in Mansfield, "Nick, you have the power to reject a $35,000 offer to burn somebody's house down," I might have agreed. But there would always have been a slight doubt there in the back of my mind until I faced that temptation. And that's just what happened late one night, just after I was released.

A couple of guys driving a Buick drove up beside me and said through one of the car windows, "Hey, Greek, how would you like to make $35,000 in about fifteen minutes?"

They wanted me to do my old thing again, set a place on fire, and five years before I would have jumped at the chance. But this time, I just looked at them, laughed, and gave them a line that was becoming a familiar part of my conversation now: "What you want me to do, stick my finger in God's eye again? God's eye is a lot bigger than mine, my friend. I like what I'm doing."

And for Nick the Greek, that was saying a lot, because what I was doing at that time was making $55.56 a week working as a counselor for a teenage drug rehabilitation program. A far cry from $35,000 in fifteen minutes, but there was no question in my mind what choice I would make.

So I went through a lot of testing in those first weeks and months out of prison, but God brought me through it all spiritually intact. Also, he showed me I had the capacity, with his help, of establishing some sort of prison ministry of my own. I wasn't sure at first exactly what such a ministry might involve. But I had plenty of help — from God and God's people — in putting together a workable concept.

Actually, my own prison ministry started long before I was released from prison, and I'm not just talking about the work I was doing preaching to inmates at the prison coffeehouse and helping out at the chaplain's office. The idea of a ministry that would reach far beyond prison walls — but would always have an ultimate purpose of bringing Christ to the cons behind bars — really got started with a series of articles that were written about me in a number of daily newspapers. As I became better known on the outside, doors opened for me to meet some of the leaders of prison ministries who could, in turn, guide me into a ministry of my own.

I've already mentioned Bill Glass, who conducted a big evangelistic crusade at Mansfield prison while I was there. He and his team led 600 people to accept Christ while they were there, and then another 600 became Christians in the follow-up program just after they left. One of the men who came with Glass was Sam Bender, a successful businessman who prayed with us in our chapel. He was a guy I liked from the first moment I met him. Another key person connected with this crusade was Watson Spoelstra, who had a real flair for publicity and for the techniques needed to get a successful ministry off the ground.

Although I was drawn to these men personally right off the bat, it took me a little longer to phase into one of their special fields of interest, namely, the American professional sports scene. Spoelstra and Bender eventually took charge of the Baseball Chapel, a Christian ministry to professional baseball players. And Glass, of course, had been old number "80" for the Cleveland Browns football team. As for me, I didn't know a thing about baseball or football. I'd never played in my life. I was out in the street cutting people up and stealing cars when the other kids were practicing their sports.

When Glass first was introduced to me, he shook my hand and said, "I really appreciate the good work you're doing in prison. And by the way, what do you think of the Cleveland Browns?"

I really didn't know what to say to him because, as I said, I didn't know a thing about football. So I just said, "I kind of like this guy named 'Scrimmage.' He seems like a pretty good football player, him and his family." I was so ignorant of the game that when they said, "Third down and four to go," I thought that meant there were three guys hurt and four who were going to be.

But even though I didn't know a thing about football, there was an immediate bond between me and these guys who were leading the crusade. Spoelstra, especially, took an interest in helping me develop my ministry while I was still in prison and then continued advising and supporting me after I got out. He noticed my mailing list was getting longer and longer while I was still an inmate. So he suggested that we put together a kind of newsletter, which he wrote, and then we mailed it out to people on the outside. We eventually started putting out one letter a month, and he would often sit me down and pick my mind on some prison-related topic, and then he'd put my thoughts together into an interesting narrative.

We continued this collaboration after I was released, and it was during one of our many brainstorming sessions together that we came up with a permanent newsletter name which eventually also became the name of my own ministry. We were trying to think up a good name, and as we tossed ideas back and forth I said "inside" — meaning the prisoners who made up the behind-bars community. He immediately responded, "Out!" And that's how we came up with the name, "Inside Out." In other words, as we've put it in a lot of our literature, "Our ministry is to the captives, inside and out."

But coming up with a name and a concept for a ministry and building a preliminary mailing list were only the first tiny steps in the work I had cut out for me. After I had begun to adjust to life on the outside again and to Satan's special ways of attacking me through my old underworld contacts and temptations, I faced the more positive challenge of taking the gospel message of inner freedom to inmates not only at

Mansfield, but also to those at many distant spots around our nation. I had come through some tough situations in my ministry at Mansfield. But my trials and tribulations there proved to be an absolutely essential training ground for what was to come. Years earlier, I had dabbled in all sorts of crime and fine-tuned my skills as a competent young mobster in my travels around the country. Finally, I had reached a level of expertise where my talents as an outlaw were highly valued by big mobsters. I was, indeed, one of Satan's most useful sons-in-law.

But now I was one of God's sons, and the question that confronted me was a little different: Did I, as a person outside the prison system, have the spiritual tools and the personal faith to enter the battle against Satan and successfully combat his hold on the nation's inmates? That was the big question that still remained to be answered.

13

The Raising
of the Dead

The majority of people in this country don't know Jesus Christ as Savior. I think every believer should be talking to nonbelievers about the faith and, when possible, lead them into a personal relationship with the Lord.

But the question is, who should you be talking to and exactly how should you go about it? You know as well as I do there are all kinds of nonbelievers: high society and skid row bums; multimillionaires and struggling young families that are barely making ends meet; super-intellectuals with a string of graduate degrees, and others who can barely read and write. Sometimes, God may lead you to people who have a completely different background from your own. He's done that with me—like the times I've spoken to professional athletes whose sports I didn't know anything about.

Once, for example, I was asked to speak to the Cincinnati Reds baseball team, and I told them right at the beginning, "I don't know a thing about baseball. The only thing I've ever done with a baseball bat is break guys' legs.'' But after admitting my ignorance, I'd try to focus in on something they could identify with: ''You are the stars of America,'' I told them. ''The kids all copy what you do. So why don't you become somebody special? Don't be like Solomon, who had a thousand women. Some of you might have five hundred women, but Solomon had many more. If he had gone to bed with one of them every day, it would have taken two-and-a-half years for him to see the same one again. What I'm trying to say to you is this: You can win the whole world, make millions of dollars and still be empty inside. There were sixteen millionaires last year who blew their brains away or OD'd. If money was the answer, why did they do it? My friends, what I'm saying to you is Jesus Christ can come and give you life and give it to you more abundantly and meaningfully. . . .''

I can relate to athletes that way, and I can get a message across to middle and upper middle-class social clubs and PTA's. But I also know, because of my special kind of upbringing and criminal experience, that God *mainly* wants me to take the gospel to the inmates and ex-cons, the guys who can best identify with my own personal experiences.

Even in a prison ministry, though, there are many ways of getting the message across. Some prison evangelists have a bigger impact on the white-collar criminals. Others go over best with other segments of the inmate population. As for me, I always zero in on the toughest guys I can find, or at least the guys who *think* they're the toughest. I know what makes these guys tick, because I was like them myself before I became a Christian.

There was this one guy named Joe in a Florida prison, and he was generally recognized as the main mafioso in that particular institution. He looked like the movie image of a godfather, even in his prison outfit, with expensive sunglasses, his shirt open halfway down his chest, and an expensive pair of shoes on his feet. I always say you can tell a person's status by the shoes he wears. The more expensive, the higher the position. Besides all this, he had a couple of bodyguards, who were also inmates, keeping close watch over him to be sure nobody rubbed him out. All the other inmates and visitors seemed afraid to get near him, but I was never scared off by appearances. I walked right up to him and said, "Hi, my name is Nick."

"My name is Joe," he said, not at all standoffish or proud, like you might expect him to be.

"Hey, Joe, do you know Jesus Christ as your Lord and Savior?" I asked. That might seem as if I were coming on a little strong, but I never stood on ceremony. Besides, he had been listening to several Christian speakers and singing groups from the evangelistic team I was with, so he knew why I was there.

Now, I came on so aggressively with Joe that I think his bodyguards started to get nervous, because they started moving in my direction. I wasn't exactly dressed like a preacher either; I was wearing an old pair of pants and an open-necked sports shirt. So I guess they might have been afraid I had slipped in to make a hit on Joe.

As I saw those guys moving toward me, I got even closer to Joe, and I walked right along with him as he headed toward the main prison building and his cell. If those guys were like most other inmates I had known, they were probably carrying a couple of ice picks under their shirts. I certainly didn't want to find one of those picks in my back before I left that place.

As it turned out, it was a good thing I stayed with Joe because by the time we had made it back to his building, he had started to cry. And by the time we made it back to his cell block, he had bowed his head and asked Jesus to come into his life. I got him set up in a Bible study before I left that day, and I continued to get letters from him months after that prison visit.

Some of the guys I've run into in prison may not have been as high up in the mob hierarchy as Joe, but they have been a lot tougher and more violent. There was this one prison I went to in Hawaii with one of Bill Glass's crusades, and the first thing I heard from the inmates was, "There are two prisoners here who run the whole place. They've even got the guards scared."

Right away, I decided those two tough nuts were the ones I wanted to meet. The prison officials tried to discourage me, but I finally convinced them to set up a meeting with those guys. I took along two inexperienced men who had just joined up with this series of crusades. As soon as we sat down with the two tough inmates, I knew their reputations were well-deserved. They really *were* tough—at least on the outside. Neither smiled at all, and they didn't sneer like young kids might do. They gave us hard looks that seemed to say, "You guys only got a couple of minutes, and then we're going to work you over." And they *could* have worked us over, too, because there weren't any prison guards nearby, and no cages or bars to separate us from one another.

I started telling them about Jesus and my faith. I didn't use a Bible at first because I wanted them to have my complete attention. But when I decided to get into the Scriptures more, and they saw me pull one out, it set one of the guys off. "You telling me, man—you mean to tell me your God can stop me from piping you?" he said.

"That's exactly what I say," I said. "My God can stop you from piping me. My God is alive."

"You wait here, and we'll just see about that!" he said, and he abruptly walked out, apparently to find a lead pipe that he could start hitting me with. The two guys who were with me weren't used to this type of evangelism, so I told them, "I think it's time for you to leave. You go and pray for me." They couldn't move fast enough.

But a few minutes later, as I sat there with one of the cons still glaring at me, not saying a word, the other guy came back — but without a pipe. That told me this so-called "tough guy" was just like all the other tough guys I'd ever met. He had a real hard surface, but if you could find a way to penetrate it, he offered no resistance at all on the inside.

So I sat down and talked openly for about twenty minutes with these two guys about Christ. I said, "I've been hard, just like you. My heart was cold. I used to foam at the mouth and my eyes would roll when somebody opened a Bible in front of me. But we all make mistakes. We all start off in some kind of prison, in special little graves that we dig for ourselves. But that's what Christ is there for — to raise us from the dead!"

Before I left, we all went down on our knees, and both of those guys committed their lives to the Lord.

Of course, I don't mean to give the impression that everybody I preach to or talk to about Christ accepts him. Many, many don't want to make that kind of commitment, that dedication of their entire lives. And it breaks my heart when they reject him.

It's hard work — almost like manual labor — to present the gospel effectively, and it's especially hard when there's an element of physical fear or tension injected into the encounter. Yet I believe some of us are called to this kind of a ministry, as personally unpleasant and even frightening as it can be at times, to confront a potentially violent person with the claims of Christ. But I've lived with violence all my life, and I guess I'm as well-prepared to meet that

213

kind of challenge as anyone. In any case, God seems to put me in situations where I have to make use of my background. And sometimes the violence I confront seems almost as threatening *outside* prison walls as it does inside.

One Sunday evening, for example, I was preaching at a quiet, peaceful little church in an Ohio suburb, when all of a sudden there was this loud crash that seemed to shake the whole building. Before anyone could check on what had happened, these three rough-looking guys burst through the front door as if they were coming into the Last Chance Saloon, looking for a fight. Their pickup truck had hit our building, and they were mad as hornets. All three were cursing at the top of their lungs, and shaking their fists at men and women alike. And people started really getting scared because these guys were obviously drunk and not entirely responsible for their actions.

One of the lay leaders in the church decided to do something about the situation, so he hopped up from his seat and said, "I have a few verses to share. The Bible says that those guilty of drunkenness will not see the kingdom of heaven. . . ." And then he started reading an appropriate passage of Scripture to prove his point.

I could see, though, that this wasn't quite the best way to handle these three characters. The well-meaning layman was just throwing kerosene on a fire that had already gotten out of hand. So I walked over to the church member, put a hand on his shoulder, and said, "Brother, will you go in the back and pray for us?"

I stopped the Bible reading at just about the right time, because the biggest of the intruders was already walking down the aisle toward me. "I kill people!" he yelled.

I looked around at the congregation, and they

seemed about ready to panic. Some looked like they were about to jump out of the nearest window. Others seemed right on the verge of attacking the tough with their Bibles. I decided to get them occupied with something more constructive, so I said, "Let's sing 'Amazing Grace,' " and I started them off.

Then I met this big guy in the center of the aisle, and I said, "What's your name?"

"My name is Bob, and I kill people!" (Sure enough, I found out later that he had killed a man at the local waterworks.)

I said, "Bob, Jesus Christ loves you!" And I uttered a silent rebuke: "Satan, they're on our territory now, ours and not yours. You have no control over them now. You have no power, and you must leave here."

Then I put my arm around Bob, but he said, "Don't you put your arm around me!" But I kept it there and walked him slowly up to the front of the church as the congregation was singing "Amazing Grace." I talked steadily to him about his past life, about his family, and finally he started to listen. He was so muscular he looked like a gorilla, and I doubted I could take him in a fair fight. But I wasn't interested in fighting with him personally. I was locked in a struggle with the powers of evil that held him in bondage.

Bob soon started softening up a little, and I told him, "Bob, I think you ought to get down on your knees right now and ask Jesus Christ to come into your life."

Sure enough, he knelt right down, and I went down beside him, and we both started to cry. "Lord Jesus, Oh Lord, I acknowledge my sin!" Bob said. "Create a new heart for me! Give me a new life! Forgive me, dear God!"

The stink from the booze on his breath was almost

too vile to stand, but somehow, the longer we prayed, it didn't matter. I knew what was going through his mind and heart at this moment because I had gone through the same thing myself. My life had bottomed out at a much lower point than his, so I could relate completely to the release he was experiencing.

After he had finished praying, he looked up at me and said, "Don't go after the other ones. They're tougher than I am."

That reminded me that we did have a couple of other ruffians back at the rear of the sanctuary. They had calmed down a little as they watched what was going on with me and Bob at the front. But they still looked as mean as ever.

So I said to Bob, "You stay here and pray to the Lord," and then I walked back to where the other two were standing. One of the guys had an ugly, bushy mustache, and I decided to try him first. "What's your name?" I asked him.

"My name is Raymond, and my father is an ordained minister, and he agrees with everything I do," he said. He was drunk too and was holding a lever that attaches to some machines used to make moonshine. "And I'm an ordained deacon," he added.

"Brother, if you've got a phony twenty-dollar bill, you've also got to have a phony master plate to make it from. I've passed phony twenty-dollar bills around myself, but I'd never try to tell you they're as good as the real thing. So no matter how phony you or your daddy might be, don't judge all Christians or God by your standards. God is still real and he cares for you, Raymond. And it's not a coincidence you came into this place. God directed your truck to hit this church. Come on up front with me and Bob," I said. Raymond followed me right up to the front, fell to his knees with Bob, and started crying too.

The congregation kept on singing "Amazing Grace" as I turned back to the last guy, a younger fellow who was looking lonely and uncertain now that his friends had left him.

"What's your name?" I asked him.

"My name is Dominic," he said. But he didn't offer any more information about himself in the same way the others had. I could tell, though, by looking at a ring on his finger that he was married.

"Dominic, my friend," I said. "How many times have you gone out with those two guys and other people on the same day you got paid? And how many times have you walked into bars and bought drinks for the house? And how many times have you sat down to drink as much as you wanted, and then gone home with most of your money spent, and then beat your wife and kids because you were angry at yourself?"

Even though I'd never met him before, I knew Dominic as well as I knew myself because I had been a lot like Dominic. I used to take my frustrations out on others when I should have been trying to change the way I was living. Dominic understood exactly what I was talking about because he started crying right on the spot. He accepted Jesus as his Savior before we even reached the front of the church where the other guys were kneeling.

Then I went on to finish my sermon, and our three new believers were sitting on the front row, even more attentive than anybody else. And they walked out of that church stone cold sober, as sober as I myself was.

There are many other stories like this I could tell you — stories about hard guys in and out of prison who respond to a certain way of presenting the gospel. But you get the point. Some people need subtle persuasion and coaxing if they're going to be led to Christ. But others need to be hit over the head with the Good

News. And that's a large part of what my mission has been and will continue to be—to hit people over the head with the fact that God loves them and wants to invite them, just as they are, with all their dirtiness and violence and roughness, into his kingdom.

Inside Out

So now maybe you know more than you ever wanted to know about Nick the Greek. I don't pretend that my life has been a pretty thing, pleasant to think or read about.

But I hope you get the main point I've been trying to make: No matter how bad or hopeless or worthless a person's life may look, God can still rescue that person and give him a decent purpose and meaning for his existence. The person by himself may not be able to change his way of living. I know it was impossible for me to pull myself up by my bootstraps. And no other human being may be able to do the job. But with God, all things are possible — even the seemingly impossible task of turning an armed robber with no concern for human life into a prison evangelist whose *every* concern is for human life.

When I was coco-butting the heads of other prisoners, setting my cell on fire, and trying to strangle the warden at that jail where I was being held before being sentenced to Mansfield, I never would have believed it if somebody had tried to tell me what direction my life would eventually take. A believer in Jesus, who was committed to helping other inmates believe? I'd have fallen over laughing if you'd told me that.

But God's ways are not our ways. So I ended up doing the last thing I ever expected to be doing. In one recent year I traveled 180,000 miles and spoke to thousands of young high school kids, college students, adults, and prison inmates about the importance of believing in Jesus Christ. Sometimes I've spoken two or three times a day, appeared on radio and television programs, and talked far into the night with individuals who wanted more in-depth information about what it means to be a Christian.

At the time of this writing, I probably spend about 70 percent of my time speaking to people outside the nation's prisons, and about 30 percent of my time communicating to those on the inside. I'd like for the percentages to be reversed, so that the inmates are getting 70 percent of my time, and I hope eventually to move in that direction because that's where my heart is, with the prisoners who often lead such a hopeless kind of existence apart from God.

But one of the reasons I spend so much time with ordinary citizens who have never darkened the door of a jailhouse is that I desperately need their help. The prisoners need their help. They need *your* help. Many of those men and women behind bars are just like I was. Even as a Christian, I was sitting in my cell week after week, month after month, getting no visits from people on the outside. Until I became better known as an inmate evangelist, I didn't even get many letters. I wrote a lot, but many times I waited in vain for a letter at mail call — a letter that somehow never seemed to come. I was fortunate because God eventually allowed me to get a little better known than most inmates, and that meant I was more likely to get cards and letters from all sorts of people. But at the same time, many of my other fellow prisoners never heard from anybody on the outside.

So that's the reason I spend so much time speaking to church groups, PTA's, colleges, and the like. I want to get them involved. And it's also the reason why I've helped set up a program called FOAP — Friend Of A Prisoner. Under this program, Christians outside the prisons can volunteer to correspond with prisoners who may be receiving very few or no letters. The volunteers just promise to send one letter a month to a specific inmate, to pray for the prisoner every night, and to remember that man or woman with a Christmas and birthday card and maybe a small gift of money on Christmas. It's not necessary for the "friends" to use their own addresses, either. They can use either their own church address or our address at Inside Out.

And now, I'm going to get very straightforward and practical with you. If this FOAP program seems to be something you might be interested in, I want you to get involved — right now. Just write to me at Inside Out, P. O. Box 29040, Parma, Ohio 44129. For that matter, even if you aren't interested in FOAP but want to know something else about our ministry, write to me at the same address. I'd love to hear from you and share with you some of the things that have happened to me since the publication of this book.

I know we've only scratched the surface in doing what Christ wants us to do to help inmates in the many prisons around this country. But that's part of the excitement of my work. I know we have a long way to go in working with prisoners, and I also know the fields are ripe for harvest. But as Jesus said, the laborers are few, so the sooner we get started on the work that remains, the better.

Jesus said, in Matthew 25:36, "I was in prison and

221

you came to visit me," and by that he meant you can, in a very real way, serve him personally when you visit and help the inmate. So take a closer look at the jails and prisons near where you live. Remember the people behind those bars on holidays and weekends, and every now and then drop in and say "hello" in the name of Christ. If you do, I can guarantee you you'll meet Jesus himself in a new and exciting way. But don't be surprised at anything that happens. Who knows, you may even find that the seed you sow will fall on fertile soil, and another unlikely soul will rise up in God's Spirit.

Remember: Even in the worst prison among the lowliest inmates, his Word will never return void!

Afterword

God keeps on working miracles.

The book you have just read is a testimony to that. After I became a Christian in prison, I craved to learn more about God. But the only Bibles we had were King James Bibles, and I couldn't understand the old English. For that matter, I could hardly read any English at all!

A fellow convict (the one whose nose I broke because he wasn't a Christian) was able to buy a Bible for two packs of cigarettes, about fifty cents, and he gave it to me. I needed a Bible like I needed a hole in the head — I had lots of Bibles, many of which had been thrown into the trash or tossed and stepped on in the hallways.

But this Bible was different. I could understand it! As I opened its pages, I was able to read God's Word in words that I used everyday. I praised God for this, and the hope grew in me that someday I would be able to meet the man who wrote this Bible version — *The Living Bible* — and who had touched so many lives with the gospel.

During the May 1973 Bill Glass crusade, I was able to speak to this man on the phone. Dr. Ken Taylor, the paraphraser of *The Living Bible*, had donated hundreds of Bibles to the crusade to be given to the prisoners. Several prisoners were selected to thank him by phone, and I was one of them. Part of my dream had come true!

After I was released from prison, many Christian publishers wanted to publish my story. But for some reason, every time a publishing deal seemed to open up, just as quickly the door closed. In one case, a deal had been all wrapped up when the publishing house hit hard times and threatened to go under.

Then one day I was in a Christian bookstore in Cleveland. I was praising God aloud, and somebody heard me—a salesman, Wendell Johnson, from Tyndale House Publishers. We talked, and he became very interested in my story.

It was through him that Tyndale House decided to publish my book and that I finally met face to face the man who had become my hero, Dr. Kenneth Taylor, president of Tyndale.

What a thrill it was for me to stand side by side with Dr. Taylor, holding in my hands the *Living Bible* that had been given to me in prison. I thank the Lord for making it possible for my book to be published by the same publisher that helped me understand God's Word in everyday English!

Praise God for the support Tyndale House Publishers has given to me and the ministry of Inside Out.